SUCE:

CW00968078

LA.

PREACHING

W. FLOYD BRESEE, PH.D.

THE MINISTERIAL ASSOCIATION
GENERAL CONFERENCE OF SEVENTH-DAY ADVENTISTS
SILVER SPRING, MARYLAND 20904-6600

Cover art modified from Communication Resources, Inc. Canton, OH 44718.
Typeset: 10/12 Palatino.

ISBN 1-57847-007-2

Published by
The Ministerial Association
General Conference of Seventh-day Adventists
Silver Spring, Maryland 20904-6600

To Ellen:
Loving companion
Faithful shepherdess
The wind beneath my wings

Contents

Introduction

If you must prepare sermons, but have had little or no training in preaching and can afford little time to prepare, this book is written especially for you. The book's principal focus is the "segment" approach to preaching. Using the segment method makes sermon preparation both simpler and faster. If you are willing to take a few hours to grasp the method, it will reward you with more interesting and effective sermons. It is hoped the book will also prove helpful to experienced speakers looking for a more efficient, time-saving way to prepare their sermons.

Beginning preachers probably have neither the interest or need to study all the details of sermon preparation and delivery. These will be abbreviated so that segment preaching can be emphasized.

The book also contains 30 sermons or sermon outlines. It is hoped these will prove helpful as "pump primers" to get you started when facing a preaching appointment. However, their principal purpose is to help you see how the book's theories are applied in a sermon.

This book often refers you to other places within the book, especially to the sermon examples in the back. These references are designated by "Section" number rather than page number. The purpose is to simplify translation and revision which invariably change pagination.

Bible quotes are from the New International Version unless otherwise noted.

Chapter 1

Why Lay Preaching?

101. Preaching Is Important

Preaching is important to Christians because it is important to Christ. My father was dying. Doctors had given up and sent him home to be with his family. He got word to each of his four children that he wanted us to come. I was living in Texas and he was in Oregon. I couldn't afford the trip, besides I was very busy. But of course I went anyway. Dad's death had first priority.

With his family around him, Dad slipped into a coma. There was nothing more we could do for him and I left to fulfill a speaking appointment 2,000 miles away. Before my assignment was completed, word came that Dad had died and the family was being called back for his funeral. By now I was really behind in my work and even less able to afford the trip. But of course I went anyway. Dad's death had first priority.

It was then that, for the first time, I really understood Jesus' words in Luke 9. He had invited a man to follow Him, but the fellow excused himself by insisting that he must first bury his father. Jesus replied, "Let the dead bury their dead: but go thou and *preach* the kingdom of God" (Luke 9:60, KJV). Jesus' words had always seemed a little heartless to me, but now I understood. He wasn't being disrespectful of family responsibilities. He was talking about priorities.

He had illustrated the importance of preaching by comparing it to a father's burial, the very thing we naturally give first priority. He had picked the thing that was the most plausible excuse possible for neglecting preaching and proclamation of His kingdom and said that that excuse was not good enough. In other words, preaching must come before everything. With Jesus, preaching had first priority.

Jesus not only taught that *we* should give preaching a high priority, it was central to *His own ministry*. Preaching, or proclaiming, is mentioned three times in His Nazareth sermon where He lays out His methods of ministry,

"The Spirit of the Lord is upon me, because he hath anointed me to *preach* the gospel to the poor; he hath sent me to heal the brokenhearted, to *preach* deliverance to the captives, and recovering of sight to the blind, to set at liberty them that are bruised, To *preach* the acceptable year of the Lord" (Luke 4:18, 19 KJV). If preaching was that central to Jesus work, it must be central to ours.

Preaching is important to church leaders because it is important to church members. A frustrated physician wrote to me on behalf of other worshipers, pleading that the one who preaches be "someone who senses the deep spiritual hunger we experience. Someone who has a kind of sensitive awareness of the devotedness of people who come to church week after week seeking food yet too often whose efforts are rewarded with scarcely crumbs. Someone impregnated with the vibrant meaning of 'feeding the flock'."

On safari in Africa, we watched from our vehicle as a pride of lions relaxed under the trees. I counted 17. Some were asleep with their legs in the air. The young were playing with one another and crawling over the adults. Why such a peaceful scene? The guide explained, "When they're full they're at peace. When they get hungry they'll kill." You see, hungry animals fight. If there's fighting going on between your church members, feed them. Hungry animals get weak and even die. If church members are growing weak or dropping out altogether, feed them. Good preaching feeds your people, keeping them strong and at peace.

Preaching is neglected by Adventists. It's not that we mean to. Historically, we have encouraged congregations to keep the pulpit at the center of the church platform to symbolize that preaching is central to our worship. But we may not have lived up to our intentions as well as we think.

My father was a Seventh-day Adventist pastor. I literally grew up in an Adventist pew, always assuming that Adventists preached more sermons than other churches, and that our preaching was somewhat superior and exceptionally biblical. Then I began work on a Master's Degree and chose for my thesis to attend the principal worship services both in Adventist and other Protestant churches. I listened to and analyzed 50 typical contemporary sermons. I was a bit shocked to learn that SDA preachers did not quote from the Bible more than the average. Adventist congregations did not use their Bibles more in worship.

Later, in conducting preaching seminars for clergy of all faiths, I often asked how many sermons their congregations expected weekly. I typically got the most votes for three—Sunday morning, Sunday night and prayer meeting. Adventist congregations may expect only one or two.

Actually, Adventism carries some built-in temptations to neglect preaching. One temptation is that our message is so exceptional we worry less about telling it well. We seem to assume that the message is so strong it isn't too serious if the telling is weak.

A second temptation results from our having a monopoly on Sabbath worship. If Sunday worshipers don't feel fed in their church they may start attending across the street at another Sunday church. Sabbath worshipers usually have no choice but us. We dislike using the word "competition" in regard to preaching. Nevertheless, human nature being what it is, a little competition tends to improve the product. Communism's failure around the world has proven dramatically that, without competition, performance deteriorates.

Preaching is rewarding. It may be the hardest work you'll ever love. The sitting down to prepare is difficult for all of us. But when you step down from the pulpit knowing that God has used you to help someone take at least a tiny step toward Jesus, you thrill with excitement and know the rewards are well worth the work.

Preaching is important. But what about lay preaching?

102. Lay Preaching Is Important

On any given Sabbath around the world perhaps as many as 80% of Adventist sermons preached are preached by lay preachers—usually, but not always, by local church elders.

All elders may not be preachers, but the Bible suggests that they should be "able to teach" (1 Tim. 3:2) and teaching is a most basic part of preaching. Paul further counseled elders, "Keep watch over yourselves and all the flock of which the Holy Spirit has made you overseers. Be *shepherds* of the church of God, which he bought with his own blood" (Acts 20:28). Elders are shepherds and a principal work of a shepherd is to feed the flock.

Lay persons have a serious *disadvantage* in preaching, for most have had little or no training. The purpose of this book is to help offset that disadvantage.

Lay persons, on the other hand, have some *advantages* over pastors when it comes to preaching. Pastors tend to move more often than most lay persons. The roots of lay persons run deeper into the congregation and thus they may understand its needs more fully and have its trust more completely. Elders have a particular advantage in that they have been chosen as leaders by the congregation. They wouldn't be elders if they didn't have people's trust. Pastors are assigned by the conference.

Pastors are paid to preach, and this alone may cause the skeptical to question what they say. Many see pastors somewhat as "saints" who live so far above and apart from the rest of the world that they don't understand everyday problems. Lay persons, on the other hand, live more like the rest of the congregation. Pastors speak *to* the congregation, lay persons speak *for* it.

Lay preaching can be effective, and it is important. Now, let's look at lay preaching in four categories: New Testament times, recent times, among women and among Adventists:

103. Lay Preaching in New Testament Times

Christianity began as a lay movement. Even Jesus did not have formal theological training. The apostles were working men whose only training was on-the-job training. Yet Jesus set them aside "that he might send them out to preach" (Mark 3:14). (See also Matt. 10:7, Luke 9:2.)

A few decades later, clergy made a sharp separation between themselves and the laity. It was eventually assumed that only clergy could be trusted to teach and preach. But the fire of Pentecost went out. Down through church history, when only clergy were presumed capable of speaking for the Lord, the church has always grown cold.

104. Lay Preaching in Recent Times

Although the sermon was central to early Christian worship, in the Middle Ages it was emphasized less and less. The Protestant Reformation reversed the trend and has brought it closer to its original New Testament place in worship.

A special emphasis on lay preaching took place in Great Britain as part of the Methodist movement. John Wesley distinguished his Methodist movement as being a preaching rather than a sacramental movement. He was at first skeptical about the effectiveness of lay preaching. But his mother took him to task and insisted he listen to some who were doing lay preaching. It changed his mind. He eventually organized great numbers of lay preachers to fill Methodist pulpits. Although they knew less theology, he felt they were effective because their's was a practical, experimental Christianity (Abbey, p. 147). Other nonconformist groups such as Baptists, Congregationalists, and even Presbyterians have made significant use of lay preachers (Turnbull, p. 462).

Some lay preachers have earned worldwide reputations. Examples would include Charles Spurgeon who never received training to preach, other than what he learned from "The Lay Preacher's Association" which he joined at age 16. He preached his first sermon that fall and became so successful, friends urged him to attend college and train for the ministry. An appointment was made for him to meet with a Professor Angus in the home of Mr. Macmillan, the publisher. Angus and Spurgeon both arrived on time but, not understanding the situation, a maid put them in different rooms of the huge house to wait. Each waited and waited for the other to arrive. Finally, patience gave out and both left. And that's as close as Spurgeon ever got to higher education or ministerial training (Day, p. 70).

Dwight L. Moody absolutely refused ministerial ordination, feeling there were advantages in remaining a lay preacher. C. S. Lewis was one of Christianity's most successful apologists and preachers. He felt that being a lay preacher helped give his message a stronger impact, especially with the skeptical (Turnbull, p. 467).

Lay preachers helped take Christianity to the American frontier. Christian Newcomer, for example, rode a Methodist circuit from his Pennsylvania farm for years prior to his ordination (Abbey, p. 147). William Jennings Bryan, one of the most eloquent speakers for and staunch defenders of Christianity and of Creationism was a lay preacher. These are just a tiny sample of thousands who, in recent times, have made a profound contribution to Christ and Christianity as lay preachers (Turnbull, p. 250).

105. Lay Preaching Women

Women have historically played an active role in the mediation of salvation. Deborah, Judith, Esther, Priscilla, Tabitha and Lydia are a few Bible examples. Paul insisted that Christ has broken down every barrier that divides people, "There is neither Jew nor Greek, slave nor free, male nor female, for you are all one in Christ Jesus" (Gal. 3:28). Romans 16 lists many women whom the Holy Spirit had called to special ministries in the early church.

But were any preachers? We know there were women prophets in the New Testament church. For example, Acts 21:9 says Philip had four "daughters who prophesied." Paul insisted that a woman must wear a head covering when she "prays or prophesies" (1 Cor. 11:5). Foley suggests, "This reference seems to indicate rather clearly that women not only spoke in the liturgical assembly but, since prophets, as we know from other early texts such as the *Didache*, offered the Eucharistic prayer and gave what we today call the sermon or homily, women prophets might well have filled these roles" (Foley, p. 66).

What reservations Paul had about women preaching were not because of some Christian standard regarding women. Rather, he did not want Christianity to become unnecessarily controversial by going contrary to standards of the surrounding society. When social standards did allow it, God reached down and picked women to speak for Him. One was Ellen White, whom he chose to be His special spokeswoman in the end time. Mrs. White never received ministerial training or ministerial ordination, yet through both pen and pulpit, God used her mightily. Who is to say the Holy Spirit cannot do the same with other lay women preachers?

106. Lay Preaching Adventists

106-A. Historically, Adventism Began with Lay Preaching

William Miller, although never a Seventh-day Adventist, is considered father of the Advent Movement. And Miller was a farmer. Born into a frontier farm family of 16 children he was able to attend school for just six years, and then only during the three winter months when farm work was slowest.

Becoming a farmer, he began teaching the Advent message as a lay preacher. Although he eventually received a license to preach, Miller never really left the farm.

Like many other lay preachers, he stubbornly resisted the call to preach. For eight years he argued with God that he was not used to public speaking, that he was not educationally qualified, that no one would listen (Knight, p. 43). But when he acquiesced, God's calling was proven, for Miller's preaching produced conversions from the very beginning.

The list of lay preachers who joined Miller in preaching the Advent message is almost limitless. Adventism began with lay preaching.

106-B. Theologically, Adventism Supports Lay Preaching

Adventists believe that every church member should have received the Holy Spirit and that everyone receiving the Holy Spirit receives some gift/s to be used in performing some ministry for Christ (1 Cor. 12:7, 11). To say we have no spiritual gift would be to say we have no Holy Spirit.

The three principal lists of spiritual gifts are found in Romans 12, 1 Corinthians 12, and Ephesians 4. Among these gifts are those most helpful to preaching: teaching, probably the primary gift for preaching; exhorting or encouraging; wisdom; knowledge; discernment and possibly even prophesying.

The purpose of spiritual gifts is "to prepare God's people for works of service, so that the body of Christ may be built up" (Eph. 4:12). Peter says that each of us is responsible for making the right use of our gifts, "Each one should use whatever gift he has received to serve others" (1 Peter 4:10). Laity given the spiritual gifts needed for preaching are responsible for using them.

It is theologically wrong and logically absurd to assume that only the clergy have been given the gifts conducive to effective preaching. It is just as wrong to assume that every pastor has all the preaching gifts.

Laity given those preaching gifts that their pastors lack are responsible for using those gifts in such a way that the church body is benefitted by every gift the Holy Spirit has placed in the congregation. No pastor is good at everything. Supportive congregations, instead of criticizing, find others in the church family who can make up for the pastor's lack by exercising the gifts the pastor was never given.

106-C. Practically, Adventism Needs Lay Preaching

The SDA church is growing as never before. It took us 107 years before our membership reached one million in 1955. Now, we are baptizing a million new members every two years. We have about 17,000 ministers available to serve approximately 9,000,000 members. When we subtract those ministers in nonpastoral positions it's obvious we don't have enough pastors to go around.

A large percentage of new Adventists are poor people in developing countries. Adventism, with its emphasis on education, hard work and clean living provides a route of upward mobility. Hopefully, in a generation or two, offspring of these new converts will be able to pay enough tithe to afford pastors, but now they really can't. Thus, their pastors must oversee huge multi-church districts and can visit a given congregation only every two or three months. Without local elders and lay preachers these churches could not survive.

Even in North America where the church is most prosperous, the majority of churches have less than 100 members and must share their pastor with sister churches. Adding it all up, we quickly realize why there is a decreasing ratio of salaried ministers per member and why more Adventist sermons must be preached by lay preachers than by clergy.

Congregations, however are becoming more and more impatient with poor preaching. People who have access to the very best professional communicators via radio and television all week are turned off by pulpit incompetence on Sabbath. Preaching that is just "filling the hour" with shallow thoughts randomly thrown together at the last minute, or that consists of the speaker reading something worshipers could as well read at home is simply not acceptable.

Lay preachers are needed, but they need to take their preaching seriously so they can preach effectively. This book hopes to help you do that. It is based on a new and simplified approach to sermon preparation that can help anyone succeed who has minimum gifts and a maximum willingness to work.

Ellen White encourages the lay preacher, "Thus the message of the third angel will be proclaimed. As the time comes for it to be given with greatest power, the Lord will work through humble instruments, leading the minds of those who consecrate themselves to His service. The laborers will be qualified rather by the unction of His Spirit than by the training of literary institutions. Men of faith and prayer will be constrained to go forth with holy zeal, declaring the words which God gives them" (*Great Controversy*, p. 606).

Chapter 2

Before Beginning

The biggest task in preaching is not preparation of the sermon but preparation of the preacher. Here are seven things you need to know before beginning your sermon preparation:

201. Know Yourself

What's your purpose in preaching? Surely it must be more than to "occupy the hour" or to "do your duty." Before studying anything else in sermon preparation we need to study ourselves. Ellen White admonishes, "When you should be studying your own heart, you are engaged in reading books. When you should by faith be drawing near to Christ, you are studying books. I saw that all your study will be useless unless you faithfully study yourself" (*Testimonies*, vol.1, p. 435).

One wrong reason for preaching is to feel important. It's amazingly, frighteningly easy for preaching to become an ego trip—usually without the preacher being aware of it. It's about the only time in life when we can do all the talking, everybody else is expected to listen and nobody is supposed to answer back. Since we speak with the authority of Scripture and church we inherit a degree of power and control over listeners. And that's heady stuff.

Preaching is not primarily proving, expounding or beautifying something. Preaching is bearing witness. It's telling something we've experienced in such a way that our listeners will experience it too.

A good talker is not necessarily a good preacher. Neither is a poor talker necessarily a poor preacher. A good preacher is one who knows and loves Christ, knows and loves people, and is willing to work hard to bring the two together. The proper purpose of preaching is to lead the listener to finally say "yes" to God. Any other purpose is out of place in the pulpit.

Are you walking the walk? Or just talking the talk? A sermon is simply the preacher up to date. It is the preacher finding exposition for his own soul.

Preaching is putting the hands of your people into the hand of God, and to do that you must have hold of both hands. No wonder Paul counseled Timothy to "pursue righteousness, godliness, faith, love, endurance, and gentleness" and to be "without spot or blame" (1 Tim. 6:11, 14).

In the long run, people are more impressed by the preaching of the very good than by that of the very able. As a lay preacher, you may not feel yourself able, but through Christ you can be good.

A Seventh-day Adventist lay preacher should be a seven-day, not just a seventh-day Christian. You can't preach with conviction and a clear conscience unless you're genuinely attempting to live during the week what you preach on Sabbath. There's nothing more humiliating than, in the middle of a sermon, to look down at your wife, your child, or a church member and realize that they know you're not living what you're preaching. Jesus preached with such power because what He taught He was. We must be what we expect our listeners to become.

Not only is character important, so is perceived character. Preaching is persuading people for Christ and there are only three means available to do that. One is logic, reasoning, the truth we present. A second is emotion or feeling. The third, and probably the most powerful, is the character of the speaker as perceived by the listener.

Little Mary comes into Kindergarten Sabbath school. Teacher has prepared a story about Jesus, along with the very latest in visual aids. The story told, Sabbath school is dismissed and Mary walks out. What has been the most effective thing in changing Mary's thinking about Jesus? Research indicates it's not the story. It's not even the visual aids. The most effective thing in changing Mary's thinking about Jesus is what Mary thought of the teacher while she told the story. Nobody is won to Christ by a person she doesn't like.

What does preaching do that reading a book can't do? Why don't we just hang a big book over the front of the pulpit and let people read it? Because preaching adds perceived character or personality. We may not intend it or even like it, but as Phillips Brooks emphasized, preaching is bringing truth through personality.

202. Know Your Lord

Christianity is Christ. Paul declares, ". . .Christ in you, the hope of glory: *Whom* we preach . . ." (Col. 1:27, 28 KJV). Christian preaching does not emphasize the preaching of a what, but of a whom. Don't preach the cross, but the Christ crucified on it. All truth is to be associated with a person, Jesus Christ.

Jesus appointed the 12 "that they might be with him and that he might send them out to preach" (Mark 3:14). The order is important. Until we have been with Him we are not prepared to preach about Him.

There's nothing harder than giving to others what you don't have, to share a Jesus you don't know. Preaching is overflowing. You cannot overflow an empty cup. When you've nothing to preach, when you dread having to do it, first look into your own soul, fill it with Jesus, then let your sermon be an overflowing. Actually, the cup that is overfilled has to overflow. When you are filled with Jesus, it is easier to speak about Him than to be quiet. You can hardly wait for your next sermon.

203. Know Your Bible

203-A. Adventist Preaching Must Be Biblical

Preaching is something we need to do with our ears and eyes before we do it with our mouths. The eyes and ears should program the mouth. With our eyes we search the Word. With our ears we listen for the needs of our people. Only then are we ready to speak. When you're assigned to preach and don't feel you have anything to say, check and you'll likely find you haven't been regularly, systematically studying your Bible.

On the other hand, if you are willing to learn, don't let a limited background in Bible knowledge discourage you from preaching. Ellen White promises, "But he who begins with a little knowledge, and tells what he knows, at the same time seeking for more knowledge, will become qualified to do a larger work. The more light he gathers to his own soul, the more of heavenly illumination will he be able to impart to others" (*Gospel Workers*, p. 98).

Paul challenged beginning preacher Timothy, ". . . I give you this charge: *Preach the Word*" (2 Tim. 4:1, 2). Chances are we all intend to be preachers of the Word, but what is biblical preaching? This is one of the easiest places to fool ourselves and, for a short time, even our congregations. Biblical preaching isn't using a lot of Bible texts. Not if we misuse them or use texts out of context. It's not even being able to quote Scripture. Not if we claim it's saying something it doesn't say.

Let's look at three prerequisites to truly biblical preaching:

203-B. Biblical Preachers Believe the Bible Works

This may seem foolishly simplistic, but it isn't. Most of us have too little confidence in the Bible as a preaching tool. Experience has made me admit to myself that I had this problem early in my own ministry. I spent many a frustrating hour leafing back and forth through my Bible trying to find something worth preaching. I wouldn't do that anymore. I now know that every passage has something exciting to say, that every practical problem of life is answered in Scripture. And if I don't find it, it's my weakness not the Bible's. I've developed an overwhelming faith in the effectiveness of the Bible as the preacher's source book.

Biblical preachers love the Bible too much to use it simply to enforce their own ideas. Two of the most important words in biblical preaching are, *"Bible first."* Unfortunately, typical preachers tend to go about it backwards. They decide what they want to say then go to the Bible to underwrite it. Unintentionally, they become their own authority and the Bible is used for the purpose of proving them right. They break the "Bible first" rule.

The magician comes out on stage and pulls a rabbit out of his hat. How does the magician manage to pull a rabbit out of his hat onstage? I'll tell you his secret. He puts the rabbit into the hat backstage. And how does the preacher get that idea out of his text in the pulpit? By putting it into his text in the study. Such backwards preaching cannot be true biblical preaching. Biblical preachers put the Bible first in their sermon preparation. They have a deep-seated belief that the Bible works.

203-C. Biblical Preachers Spend Time with the Bible

Every preacher needs a regular, systematic Bible study program. Finding time for it is hard for every preacher, and doubly hard for the lay preacher. Life is a continuous struggle to keep the urgent from crowding out the important.

Variety stores sometimes used to hang a sign in the window, "Dry goods and notions." Unfortunately, preachers who don't persistently pursue Bible study may as well hang that sign over their pulpits. "Dry goods," old ideas everybody's already heard a hundred times. "Notions," shallow ideas off the top of the preacher's head. Ellen White warns, "It is a sin to be neglectful of the study of the Word while attempting to teach it to others" (*Gospel Workers*, p. 99).

Paul counsels, *"Study* to shew thyself approved unto God, a workman that needeth not to be ashamed, rightly dividing the word of truth" (2 Tim.2:15, KJV). But that word "study" is unpopular with many of us. As we sometimes say, there is no expedient to which the human mind will not go to avoid the real labor of thinking.

Leadville, Colorado was a busy mining town when one mine owner found his mine had run out of ore. He salted it with a little ore planted here and there and went looking for a sucker to buy it. And he found one. It didn't take the new owner long to realize he'd been a fool. But he was a working fool. With pick, shovel and bucket he began digging. Straight down he went. Thirty feet down he struck one of the richest veins of ore in all the Rocky mountains.

Too many preachers stay on the surface of Scripture and preach shallow ideas that have already been mined out. Somehow, we must dig a little deeper. Rich veins are always there. And when we don't dig, it isn't likely so much because we're busy or incapable, but because digging is simply hard work. But keep your courage up in the digging process by reminding yourself of the fun of finding.

203-D. Biblical Preachers Apply the Bible to Themselves

They never open the Bible without breathing a prayer that the Holy Spirit who gave the Word will interpret and apply it to their own lives. They plead that God will speak to them before He speaks through them to others. They approach the Bible story as participants not just spectators. They interpret the Bible as it applies here and now, not just back there then. They first approach the Bible, not to find something to say to others, but something that changes them.

One of the best ways to do this, and at the same time create a backlog of sermon ideas, is journaling. As you study Scripture, write in your journal ideas and applications meaningful and exciting to you. The beauty of it all is that when you come back to your journal looking for something to preach, you'll be surrounded by ideas that truly interested you. And therein lies a great secret to interesting sermons. For we interest others by that which exceedingly interests us.

204. Know Your Tools

Your primary preaching tool is, of course, the Bible. Other books, especially those written to help us study the Bible, can be very helpful. They can save us from misinterpreting the Scripture. They can stimulate our thinking about it. However, they can never be more than aids. Even the best of them cannot replace our own direct cross-examination of our passage and its cross-examination of us.

204-A. Bible Versions

As older Bible manuscripts are discovered and as language develops, new Bible versions are continually being published. We ought not be afraid of using them if they can really help us understand the Word. Ellen White had a pastoral concern for persons who felt comfortable only with the older versions. However, she made considerable use of newer ones. For example, in *Ministry of Healing,* she quoted from four versions other than the King James, and she quoted from those four versions some 69 times.

All recognized Bible versions seek to communicate the meaning of the original manuscripts. Versions whose emphasis is not only on meaning, but also on the linguistic form of the original language are called *formal.* Versions whose primary emphasis is on meaning, with only a secondary emphasis on linguistic form are called *dynamic* or idiomatic. Translations having almost total emphasis just on meaning, are called *paraphrases.*

Which Bible version is best? It depends on your purpose. Some are best for study, others for reading in church, others for children and still others for the biblically illiterate. The good news is that the plan of salvation can be found in any of them. We'll look at a few of the better known English versions readily available:

King James Version, 1611. The Greek manuscripts from which the King James Version was translated, were all copied a thousand years or more after the Apostles. It does not have the advantage of older, more accurate manuscripts discovered since its publication. However, many Christians are used to and attracted by its classic, old English language. Never belittle a Bible stained through with a thousand sweet memories of bright religious experiences out of one's past.

New King James Version, 1979. This updating of the old King James modernizes the language, but it is based on the same Greek text as the 1611 version and does not take advantage of older manuscripts discovered since that time.

Revised Standard Version, 1952. This version aims to keep as close as possible to the King James, except where the language is antiquated and where the manuscripts from which the King James was taken have since proven to be inaccurate. It is a formal translation as near to a literal translation as the English language allows. A good study Bible.

New Revised Standard Version, 1989. This more recent version of the RSV attempts to remove gender bias from Scripture.

Jerusalem Bible, 1966. This is a Roman Catholic translation and includes the apocryphal books. It results from the highly respected scholarship of the School of Biblical Studies in Jerusalem.

New American Bible, 1970. This Bible is a product of American Roman Catholics and includes the apocrypha. It is clear, simple, straightforward and generally accurate.

New American Standard Bible, 1971. This translation is a meticulous word-for-word reproduction in English of the original language. Being a very formal translation it is strong in Greek, but weak in English. An excellent study Bible, but with a somewhat stilted style.

New International Version, 1978. This version was prepared by a large team of international scholars representing most of the chief Protestant denominations. It is a conservative translation that preserves most standard theological terms. Its first concern is accuracy and fidelity to the thought of the biblical writers.

Today's English Version, 1966. This dynamic version is sometimes called the Good News Bible. Designed to be used by those for whom English is a second language, simplicity and readability were considered more important than literary quality. Thus, it tends to be shunned by scholars because of its use of simple language. However, it quite accurately presents the real meaning of the Greek in the most uncomplicated structure possible.

New English Bible, 1970. This dynamic Bible is written in British English. It was designed for non-church-goers and youth in England. Written for a literary audience, it is sometimes called the elegant version. It is not a good Bible for detailed word study.

Phillips Modern English Translation, 1958. This is really a biblical paraphrase, interpreting the original very freely. However, it sometimes helps bring obscure passages to life.

Living Bible, 1971. Like Phillips, this is a one-man paraphrase. It was prepared by Kenneth Taylor, a seminary-trained businessman. It resulted from his experiments with his own devotions with his children. It is written in a style easy to understand, but its accuracy and faithfulness to the original documents are frequently in doubt.

Amplified Bible, 1964. This is not so much a translation as a biblical storehouse offering several alternative renderings for significant words. Interpretative paraphrases are added in brackets. This is not a very readable Bible, but a useful tool for study.

If you have access to them, having several versions is helpful, but how do you use them in sermon preparation? It's probably best to begin with the version you're going to use in the pulpit. This should likely be one of the more formal translations and must be one acceptable to the large majority of your listeners. Do most of your study in the formal versions. The paraphrases may help you get new insights, but be cautious about depending on them or using them in the pulpit.

One of the best and simplest ways to use versions is to have a parallel Bible. On a given page, a parallel Bible will have your passage in one version in the first column, another version in the second column, etc. You may be able to read your passage from half a different versions right on the same page. You can quickly see how the same original word or phrase was translated by each. For the lay preacher with no access to the original Bible languages this is one of the simplest and most accurate ways to ascertain the original writer's intent.

204-B. Bible Reference Books

If you can have but one reference book it should probably be a **concordance.** You can look up a word from a text or topic that comes to mind and the concordance will tell you where it's found in the Bible. If your library must be limited you'll take courage from the story of a minister who went to visit William Miller, only to find he was not at home. Asking Miller's daughter for the privilege of seeing Miller's library, the minister was shown only two books, the Bible and Cruden's Concordance. From that limited library Miller studied out the truths of the Advent Movement.

Bible encyclopedias give great gobs of information about Bible times, people and places.

Bible dictionaries define and enlarge on Bible words or terms.

Topical Bibles are an excellent tool, especially for topical sermons. For example, if you wanted to preach on the Second Coming of Christ, you wouldn't even find the term used in a concordance, for the Bible doesn't use those specific words. But a topical Bible looks at Bible topics, not just Bible words and would list a host of texts under Second Coming.

Bible commentaries will take a text and enlarge on its principal words or phrases. Any lay preacher with a Bible and nothing else but the *Seventh-day Adventist Bible Commentary* has access to more preaching material than he or she could ever use. If you have a computer, but not many religious reference works, investigate buying software that includes Bible versions, commentaries, etc.

204-C. Ellen White Books

Have as complete a library of Ellen White's writings as you can afford. The Conflict of the Ages series makes a good beginning for such a library. I would urge every lay preacher to have *Christ's Object Lessons*. Each chapter heading gives the text for a parable. Study it carefully in your Bible then read her chapter and you have more than enough material for a sermon. The 29 chapters provide source material for 29 sermons on Jesus' parables. *Mount of Blessings* can be used in a similar way to prepare a sermon series on applied Christianity from the Sermon on the Mount.

If you have many Ellen White books you may need to purchase an index to her writings. Better still, if you can afford it, get *Ellen G. White Writings on Compact Disc* for your computer, an outstanding research source. For example, you could type in the word "preaching", press a button and your screen would display every paragraph in which the word is used in her published writings.

In many countries a few years ago, no male preacher was properly dressed for the pulpit unless he wore a vest. On the other hand, it was also improper for his coat to be unbuttoned. Thus, his vest barely showed. The Spirit of Prophecy books are like the vest. The Adventist preacher should hardly enter the pulpit without having studied what Ellen White has said about his passage or topic. However, like the vest, her writings should not be overly obvious in the pulpit.

Mrs. White was directly asked how she would recommend her writings be used in preaching. Her counsel came in three parts: first, begin your study in the Bible and stay there until you have gleaned everything you can. Second, see what light her books shed on your passage. Third, go into the pulpit and preach from the Bible!

I would discourage taking her books into the pulpit. Several bad things happen. People see you as too lazy to have prepared well. They cringe at the possibility of your reading long passages. And they tend to fear they're about to be spanked.

We brought a little puppy into our home and began the process of housebreaking her. Someone said the best procedure was to roll up a newspaper when she made a mistake and swat her with it. We did, and it worked. But to her dying day she hated newspapers so much she ran behind the couch every time anybody picked one up. You see, we never learn to like the thing with which we're spanked. When we use Ellen White to spank congregations or kids, we shouldn't be surprised if they never learn to like her. Use positive, short, pithy, inspiring quotes in the pulpit and listeners will be trained to appreciate the wise counsel God has given His church through her.

204-D. Miscellaneous Books

Any worthwhile, thought-provoking books are helpful in sermon preparation. Important as it is to read the Bible and other religious works, it is also worthwhile to read some secular materials to keep ourselves contemporary and our preaching practical.

However, basing a sermon on some book other than the Bible is questionable at best. Remember those two words so basic to preaching, "Bible first." All Adventist preaching must be Bible-based and if it didn't originate in the Bible, if your first and primary study in sermon preparation was in some other book and the Bible was an afterthought, it is a backwards sermon.

Books of sermons can be helpful, especially for the beginner, but they should be used sparingly. They may produce ideas around which you may form your sermon, or even a framework for it. But a sermon is as personal as a toothbrush. You ought to use your own.

One problem with using miscellaneous books is that in the midst of sermon preparation you don't have time to read many books. Ideally, read books ahead of time and write on the flyleaf ideas you might want to use in a sermon. Better yet, start a topical file in which to store them. It can be as simple as a cardboard box or as complicated as a computer. A good file can supply 50 to 75 percent of your sermon. But a file must include a fairly complete index. When you want to file something and can't find a place to file it, you give up on filing.

205. Know Your Preparation Takes Time

You can be taught to preach, but only if you're willing to learn. You can learn to preach well, but only if you're willing to work hard. It is a tragic presumption on the work of the Holy Spirit to assume that He will fill your mouth in the pulpit with what you have not taken time to learn in the study. As Emerson said, "You can have truth or repose. You cannot have both."

How much time should it take to prepare a sermon? The old rule of thumb is one hour in study for one minute in the pulpit. Realistically, most preachers probably spend 10 to 20 hours preparing a 30 minute sermon. A beginning lay preacher should likely take longer. If you preach regularly you likely don't have that kind of time. On the other hand, if you don't have to preach weekly but spend a little sermon preparation time every week, by the time your turn comes to preach you'll have racked up considerable preparation hours.

Think now and then, not of the precious time you spend preparing, but of the time your audience spends listening. If you preach a 30 minute sermon to 50 people you have taken 25 hours of their time. See that their time isn't wasted.

205-A. Take Time to Pray

Sermon preparation should begin on our knees praying the preacher's prayer, "Lord, what do *you* want me to say?" Authority for preaching comes less from the classroom than from the prayer room. Pray before your open Bible and ask for the Holy Spirit who gave it, to give you something from it for His people.

205-B. Start Early

One of the best secrets to preparing a worthwhile sermon, especially effective illustrations and practical application, is to start early. Do your Bible study and reading long before your preaching date. Keep at it until you feel you know about what God wants said. Now go about your other duties. Let the sermon wander through your mind, floating somewhere between the conscious and subconscious. Here are three dramatic rewards of starting early:

1. It eases the pressure and lets the creative juices flow. Creativity despises deadlines. The brain's filing system tends to jam when pressed too hard. But if you take the pressure off, it may produce profusely.
2. It saves time. Instead of gazing at the ceiling trying to come up with practical applications or poring over books looking for illustrations, let them come out of your week. Your sermon will grow while you're doing other things.
3. It makes your sermon practical and interesting. Sermons that grow out of the present fit the present. Sermons that come from everyday life meet everyday needs.

205-C. Plan Yearly

If you preach often, it's a good idea to sit down annually to review last year's sermons and plan your preaching for the upcoming year.

Yearly planning saves time. It takes much less time than what you would spend through the year if you depended on picking sermon topics out of the air helter-skelter. I'm ashamed to admit it, but in my early years I occasionally paced the floor late into the night just before I was to preach, still not certain of what my subject should be. With the time wasted on the last minute struggle to find something to preach, we could prepare masterpieces!

Yearly planning produces balanced preaching. If you love your people you want to provide them with spiritual food that's not only tasty and nutritious, but also balanced. Broccoli is highly nutritious, but if you ate nothing else, you would probably die of malnourishment. When you've been feeding your people a diet based just on whatever came to mind, or what you happen to like best, the process of reviewing last year's sermons will force you to confront the fact and encourage you to plan future sermons that provide a balanced diet.

205-D. Get Help

One unusual way to save time in sermon preparation is to recruit others to work with you. Sometimes a spouse can help with the research. If you lead out in prayer meeting, try discussing your passage there and ask the people what they think it says and what it means today. Get together in a small group atmosphere with friends, maybe on a Sabbath afternoon, and ask for their insights on your passage or topic.

Preparation of an effective sermon takes great gobs of time. Poor lay preaching results, not so much from inability to preach, as from inability to find adequate preparation time. The busy lay preacher must grasp every means available to help save the most preparation time possible. The segment approach to sermon preparation outlined in the next two chapters will help.

206. Know Your Sermon Type

The lay preacher need not be interested in a lot of homiletic theory. Why then is it important to know the different sermon types before beginning sermon preparation? One reason is so that your sermons will have more variety. God did not make the sky all blue, or the rainbow of just one color. Nobody plants only one color in a flower garden. People like variety, and if some of your sermons are of one type and some of another it helps prevent boredom.

Also, you begin preparation differently depending on the type of sermon you plan to preach. You start with a Bible passage, a Bible topic, a Bible character or a Bible verse depending on whether your sermon is to be expository, topical, biographical or textual. Let's look at definitions, strengths and potential weaknesses of each of those four sermon types. I'll begin with the type we should probably favor most and work toward the one we usually favor least.

But first we need to assert again that all Adventist preaching must be biblical. No one of the four types we'll look at is necessarily more biblical than the others. Making a sermon biblical depends less on the sermon type than on how the sermon is prepared.

The preparation of every sermon should *begin* in Scripture. The preaching of it can then begin anywhere—preferably with the congregation. Having found Bible truth, the preacher may well begin the sermon by awakening the listener's interest in and need for that truth. Beginning the sermon delivery with the Bible doesn't make a sermon biblical. Beginning the sermon preparation with the Bible does.

206-A. Expository

Definition. Simply and somewhat arbitrarily defined, an expository sermon is a sermon that's based on the exposition (or explanation) of three or more verses of Scripture. If the passage discussed is shorter than that, the sermon is usually called textual. Often the unit of Scripture is a paragraph, at other times a chapter, occasionally an entire book.

Section 502 in the back of this book exemplifies a sermon that's expository in the strictest sense, in that the sermon simply follows the order of the passage. This is not essential, but somewhat typical. Section 503 has an expository sermon based on four chapters at opposite ends of the Bible—Genesis 1, 2 and Revelation 21, 22. Section 504 shows an expository sermon that gives highlights from the entire book of Ecclesiastes. Outlines exemplifying expository sermons are in Sections 511, 512, 513, 515, 516 and 517.

Strengths. Expository preaching has much to commend it and, if properly used, is probably the best kind of preaching for most lay preachers. It is usually quite biblical, inclining the preacher to truly study the mind of the Bible author. It generally contains good depth and affords an inexhaustible supply of material. It tends to lead to balanced preaching, because the topics come from Scripture rather than out of the preacher's head. It may actually be the easiest to research, because you can focus on just one passage, digging deeply enough to truly master it and feel quite confident about its meaning.

Potential weaknesses. Expository preachers are tempted to emphasize explanation over application. As Spurgeon used to say, "The sermon begins where the application begins." Spend some time on what your passage says or means, but much time on what difference it makes. Don't make your congregation spend the whole morning in ancient Palestine. None of them live there during the week.

Seldom does a Bible passage concentrate exclusively on a single point—or even on one subject. Too many expository preachers begin by heading north toward one point, then turn and go south toward another for a while. Finally, they throw in a little east and west and sit down with the audience still going round in circles. Avoid this by studying your passage until the Holy Spirit convicts you with one basic truth most obvious in the passage or most needed by your congregation. Then focus your exposition on this truth and pass over everything extraneous to it.

206-B. Topical

Definition. A topical sermon is one in which a subject is chosen and the Bible as a whole is researched on that subject. The content and form owe more to the topic than to any one passage of scripture. Topical preachers usually begin their sermon by choosing a topic and then developing it in depth with the aid of a topical Bible or concordance. Sample topical sermons are found in Sections 508 and 509. Additional outlines are in 521, 522, 524 and 525.

Strengths. Properly prepared, a topical sermon may be more biblical than its expository counterpart. To understand what Scripture says on a subject, turning to one passage or book is not enough. It requires the perusal of the whole Bible—the topical approach. Hence we are safest in following Isaiah's "here a little, there a little" counsel (Isa.28:10) and searching all the Scriptures. For example, to obtain the right balance between faith and works from the book of James alone is pretty difficult. But put James with Paul, as a topical sermon ought to do, and we have balanced truth.

Speaking of Bible authors, Ellen White explained: "One writer is more strongly impressed with one phase of the subject; he grasps those points that harmonize with his experience or with his power of perception and appreciation; another seizes upon a different phase; and each, under the guidance of the Holy Spirit, presents what is most forcibly impressed upon his own mind—a different aspect of the truth in each, but a perfect harmony through all. And the truths thus revealed unite to form a perfect whole, adapted to meet the wants of men in all the circumstances and experiences of life" (*The Great Controversy*, p. vi).

Although expository sermons can be doctrinal (see Sections 519 and 520), when topical preaching is neglected doctrinal preaching tends to be neglected too. And when we stop preaching Adventist doctrine we'll stop having Adventist audiences, for the doctrines that make SDA Christians will keep them SDA Christians. Preaching "love alone" brings a truth we desperately need, yet separate it from basic Adventist beliefs and we produce generic Christians and disappointed congregations. A good rule of thumb is to preach every Adventist doctrine to every Adventist congregation every three years. But be sure to make those doctrines practical and contemporary. To say that our beliefs aren't contemporary would be to say Adventism is obsolete and superfluous. We see our doctrines as applying to some time long ago only if we stopped studying them in depth a long time ago.

Topical preaching lends itself most naturally to the Christian year, which requires topics such as Mother's Day, Christian Education, Missions Promotion, Stewardship, Communion, etc.

Potential weaknesses. Topical preaching has the reputation of not being biblical because the preacher has researched everything under the sun on the subject and not emphasized Bible research. Remember, all Adventist preaching must be biblical.

Topical preaching may also lead to using texts out of context, for you don't have time to study the entire context and setting of each verse used. I would suggest that topical preaching is not necessarily less biblical, but it is necessarily more difficult, because each text must be studied in its context lest we use it to say something it wasn't meant to say.

206-C. Biographical/Narrative
Definition. Biographical/narrative preaching normally centers on the story of a Bible character or incident. Narrative preaching typically places the story

in a contemporary setting, with the preacher sometimes telling it in the first person. Biographical preaching is closely related but usually places the story in the setting in which the Bible character lived. Section 526 has a biographical sermon outline on Moses, 506 is an expository sermon summarizing the book of Hosea, but the final division shifts to the narrative.

Strengths. Ellen White wrote, "As an educator no part of the Bible is of greater value than are its biographies" (*Conflict & Courage*, p. 10). Biographical/ narrative preaching is preaching most like the way Bible writers wrote. They were master storytellers, as was Jesus. The Bible is made up principally of narration. It features stories of people and places, not just theological theories and rational arguments. The Bible is approximately 90% narration, while most sermons are about 90% exhortation.

Biographical/narrative preaching is practical. It emphasizes religion, not as theory, but as it's lived. This, of course, tends to make it exceptionally interesting.

Potential weaknesses. The biographical/narrative sermon's appealing story form can also be its greatest danger. Listeners may go away only entertained and not enlightened.

Actually, it's not as easy to make this type of sermon interesting as we might presume, especially for the Adventist audience that's already heard the story of Paul on the road to Damascus 100 times. It takes some careful research and some deep thinking to make an old story fresh.

Biographical/narrative preaching is subtle. It tends to convey its spiritual lessons implicitly rather than explicitly. You can easily be fooled, for the audience may not be learning what you think you're teaching.

This sermon type is often too general. For example, the life of Moses teaches the lasting results of a mother's training, or the tragedy of impatience or how to accept criticism. The best sermons focus on one main lesson and the biographical/narrative preacher needs to decide what that single focus will be. Every hunter knows you bring down more big game with a rifle bullet that penetrates and kills than a half-dozen pellets from a shotgun that just irritate a bit and have too little impact to get under the skin.

To make this sermon type work, start with *facts*. Begin with the biblical facts. Find out everything the Bible has to say about the person or incident. Then add historical facts. Learn all you can about the times with which the account deals. Only then do you want to add an informed imagination. Jesus did, in His story of the rich man and Lazarus. But make sure your imagination does not violate the biblical and historical facts. And when you put it all together be sure the lesson you teach is the lesson the Bible teaches.

206-D. Textual

Definition. The textual sermon is one based on only one or two verses of Scripture. The sermon in Section 510 is a textual sermon based on Acts 1:8, a

Bible verse so full of meaning it can deserve a whole sermon. Section 529 outlines a Communion sermon. It's easier to preach a textual Communion sermon, because the sermon is shorter and one or two texts may yield as much as you have time to say.

Strengths. Because your passage is short the sermon may be simpler and easier to understand, driving home a single idea. Typically, the outline or organization of the textual sermon comes directly from the text. Thus, it may be easier to organize.

Potential weaknesses. I've purposely put this sermon type last because it tends to be least biblical. Not many Bible verses lend themselves to it. Too often it is a "springboard sermon," using the Bible merely as a starting point from which the preacher sails into the stratosphere of his own notions. Expanding 15 words from scripture into 5,000 words from the preacher isn't conducive to truly biblical preaching.

206-E. Combinations

At times your sermon may end up with some parts being expository, some topical, and some biographical/narrative. There's nothing wrong with that. Section 507 illustrates with a sermon where the first division is expository and the rest topical. Sample outlines of combination sermons are in sections 514 and 523.

There is significance, however, in whether you **begin** your preparation by investigating a passage, a topic, or a narrative. Thus, you must settle the type of sermon you **intend** to preach before you begin preparing.

If you have always used just one of the sermon types, I urge you to experiment with others. You may find one that fits you better. Form preaching habits that are effective, not just comfortable. Keep experimenting to keep growing.

207. Know the Segment Method of Sermon Preparation

I was feverishly working on my doctoral dissertation on the teaching of preaching. It was a fun project traveling across the country interviewing the 16 persons chosen by their peers as the most outstanding teachers of preaching in the United States. I spent several hours listening to each one. They emphasized how the preparation of a sermon seemed so complicated to most beginners, and that we needed to find a simpler way. Out of that experience grew the Segment Method of sermon preparation, the core and uniqueness of this book.

One advantage of the Segment Method is simplified sermon preparation. Sitting down to prepare an entire sermon is an awesome task. But to prepare a few sermon segments isn't nearly so frightening.

A second advantage is that the Segment Method guarantees biblical sermons. It begins with and centers on Scripture.

A third advantage is that it produces interesting sermons. Each segment includes illustration or practical application. Thus, these are worked all through the sermon and are never more than a few minutes apart.

207-A. Segments Defined

A sermon segment is a somewhat self-contained portion of a sermon. Like the compartments of a ship, each segment is somewhat self-contained yet joined to the whole. When preached, a segment is likely about two to five minutes in length. Put half a dozen segments together that are related both to one another and to one basic theme and you have the body of a sermon. Add an introduction and conclusion and your sermon is ready.

Don't begin by worrying about preparing a successful sermon. If you can just prepare some good segments you can preach a good sermon. Sermon segments divide a big, overwhelming task into simple, understandable steps.

207-B. Segment's Three Parts

The segment's three parts are lesson, proof and illustration/application.

Segment lesson. The segment lesson is the spiritual truth you want your listener to learn and follow. It must express a point of view. It's not just the subject of your segment, but what you're going to say about it.

Segment proof. Usually your lesson and the proof for it will come to you together. The proof should nearly always come from the Bible. Only occasionally should it be from Mrs. White, a secular source, or reasoning alone. Sociological or philosophical discourses, with the Bible scarcely opened, will not feed the soul or produce revival and reformation.

Please be patient with my emphasizing again that the truly biblical sermon does not just include the Bible, it begins with the Bible. Biblical preachers come to the Bible first in their sermon preparation. As nearly as possible, they come with a blank mind, knowing nothing but their passage or topic. They do not open the Book looking for something that agrees with what they want to say. They open it to find what it wants them to say. In the pulpit, use the lesson-proof order of things, but in your research, shun it like the plague.

Preaching must never be authoritarian, but it must always be authoritative. A cartoon pictures two ministers standing in a large church sanctuary. The worship service is about to begin but only two worshipers are present. One minister says to the other, "I told you it wasn't wise to end each sermon with, 'But what do I know?'" Preaching without authority doesn't attract.

The Bible is not only your source book, it is the source of your authority. As a lay preacher you may feel you speak with very little authority. Your listeners may feel it too. But when what you say comes from the Bible that your listeners do consider an authority, its authority becomes yours and Bible believers will listen with respect.

When you begin biblically, you have an inexhaustible supply of sermon material. Having published more than 3,000 sermons, Charles Spurgeon declared, "After 35 years I find that the quarry of Holy Scripture is inexhaustible. I seem hardly to have begun to labor in it."

When you begin biblically, you don't get bored with your preaching. Why? Because you are continually learning rather than continually repeating over and over what you already know.

Now, as you study your passage you'll come across a verse or word that contains an inspirational thought. That thought, truth or spiritual verity is what we mean by "lesson." The Bible verse or word is your "proof." You have two of the three parts of your segment.

Segment illustration\application. The purpose of preaching is to relate Scripture to what is happening now. Preaching is bridge building. It builds a bridge from the past to the present, from the Scripture to the street, from the Savior to the sinner. No bridge works unless it's firmly anchored on both ends. The secret of successful preaching is to emphasize both what God wants and what mankind needs.

Good preaching is a message from God applied to the needs of people. God loves people, not just abstract truth. His truth is always for the purpose of helping people. If your message doesn't help people it's hardly real truth.

If available, see how Bible commentaries, Ellen White's writings, and other Christian authors apply your passage to practical Christian living. Use current events, nature, and experiences in your own life to make your sermons relevant to life as your listeners live it.

Illustration and application are intimately related. Not every lesson needs an illustration, but every one needs an application and a good illustration is often the best way to apply your lesson to life.

The best illustrations come from typical life situations. When they do, they are so practical that further application is sometimes hardly necessary. If your illustration is about a knight going into battle you may need to take some time afterward to show how the idea, proof, and illustration apply to contemporary life. But when you tell of your impatience when trying to get your children to bed at night, the application may well be right in the story.

Parts one and two (lesson and proof) of your sermon segments will almost certainly come whenever you prayerfully apply yourself to the seat of the chair and your eyes to the page of Scripture. Part three (illustration/application) often comes only as you go through the week living your normal routine with these lessons continually in the back of your mind.

Whenever you have the lesson and proof but can't come up with the illustration/application it's probably because of one or more of the following reasons: (1) you haven't developed the habit of seeing sermons in everyday life; or (2) the lesson is not practical enough, not closely related to life; or (3) you've not had the lesson long enough to take it with you into enough life situations. You didn't start preparing early enough.

People need Bible truth most. Unfortunately, they like stories best. So what do we do? Nobody gets any good out of a lesson and proof they don't hear, so there's no use ignoring the importance of holding their attention. On the other hand, we don't want to be storytelling preachers, for God doesn't call us to be entertainers. An advantage of the lesson, proof, illustration/application segment is that your sermon keeps moving from one to the other.

They tell the story of a musician commissioned to compose a piece for his king. Knowing from experience that the king usually fell asleep at concerts, the musician wrote the music accordingly. During the concert, as the music played softly, the king's eyes grew heavy and his head began to nod. But just then came a loud clashing of cymbals that shocked him awake. Again quiet music. Again sleep beckoned. Again the music wakened, this time with a double fortissimo.

Segment preaching uses the same technique. It offers a couple of minutes of lesson and proof (careful reasoning), followed by a couple of minutes of illustration/application (storytelling), followed by lesson and proof from the next segment, etc. Enough illustration so they'll hear, enough lesson so they're helped.

207-C. Sample Segments

Actually, the Segment Method is just simplified common sense. Here's a sample segment as you might preach it in a sermon:

Lesson: Every physical (human) refuge eventually fails.

Proof: Psalm 46:2, 3, "Therefore we will not fear, though the earth give way and the mountains fall into the heart of the sea, though its waters roar and foam and the mountains quake with their surging." Whenever a significant Bible word is mentioned more than once in a short passage we expect it to be important. Notice that mountains are mentioned twice. Mountains are nature's fortresses, immovable, unshakable. The Psalmist is asking, "What will you do when the unshakable shakes?"

Illustration/application: Every physical, every human refuge eventually fails. I know a father who loved to throw his baby into the air. Every time he went up, the baby laughed. Every time he came down, father caught him—except once. His little head hit the concrete and he never laughed again. Every human refuge eventually fails. Some refuge has failed, some hurt is pressing on every heart here: the death of a loved one, a loveless marriage, a child who's left the Lord, health that is failing, work that isn't working. But "God is our refuge." No wonder this psalm led Martin Luther to write, "A mighty fortress is our God, A bulwark never failing." Every physical (human) refuge eventually fails—but Jesus never fails.

Turn now to Section 502, I-B and see how this segment is used in a sermon. In fact, notice that each subdivision (marked A, B, etc.) of the sermon is made up of a sermon segment. In 503, on the other hand, each main division (I, II, etc.) is basically a sermon segment. Please look through several sermons and outlines in the back of the book to see various ways segments are used.

Usually, proof-lesson-illustration/application is the best order for a segment. Occasionally, it lends variety and works best to change the order. Notice that 505 uses a proof-lesson-illustration/application order. In Section 508, I-D uses an illustration/application-proof-lesson order.

The point is that, in preparing sermon segments, always think in threes. As you study your Bible, continually be looking for a lesson, a proof and an illustration/application. Preach them in that order unless you have an instance in which another order simply makes more sense.

207-D. Rules for Good Segments

Here are six rules for preparing effective segments:

Rule 1. The lesson must be true. We never mean to be unbiblical or to preach something that's untrue. The problem is that, in our attempt to come up with something original and fresh, we get carried away and wind up preaching plausibility as new light. Do not preach your private interpretation of Scripture, or speculative truth. Never allow your own pride of discovery to undermine the faith of your listeners. Whenever you come up with an idea totally different from anyone else's, don't deny the gnawing suspicion that it may be because they knew better.

Sister White counsels, "There are a thousand temptations in disguise prepared for those who have the light of truth; and the only safety for any of us is in receiving no new doctrine, no new interpretation of the Scriptures, without first submitting it to brethren of experience. Lay it before them in a humble, teachable spirit, with earnest prayer; and if they see no light in it, yield to their judgment; for in the multitude of counselors there is safety" (*Testimonies*, vol. 5, p. 293).

Rule 2. The lesson must be important. First, it is not enough that your lesson is true, it must also be important. The apostle Peter was a married man. It's true, but not a big, significant idea and not likely very important to your congregation.

Second, it must be a lesson—not just what you're going to talk about, but what you're going to say about it. Never just a topic, always a point of view, and hopefully one that contains some depth of thought. Not "The nature of sin," but "Sin destroys, God's love restores." Not "Christ deals with sin," but "Christ frees from both the penalty and the power of sin." Not "Health reform," but "God wants us to be healthier so we can be happier." Not "The importance of right attitudes," but "Right actions do not guarantee right attitudes, but right attitudes do guarantee right actions."

Rule 3. The lesson must be interesting. True, important lessons are not enough. Lessons should also be fresh, contemporary, practical, interesting. To say the greatest truths in the same old mundane way can be boring. Some examples: not "God is love," but "God's love is not passive, but aggressive." Not "God can give us His Holy Spirit," but "God will fill us with His Holy Spirit to whatever extent we let Christ empty us of sin." Not "We ought to join the church," but "Christ gave us the church so that, surrounded by loving Christians, we can learn to love Christ."

Rule 4. The proof must directly prove the lesson. Never use a verse as proof unless it makes a clear, direct case for your lesson. Let's illustrate with John 3:16, "For God so loved the world that he gave his one and only Son, that whoever believes in him shall not perish but have eternal life." You could use this verse to prove that "Love leads to giving" ("God so loved . . . that he gave), or that "God loves everybody" ("God so loved the world). You have direct proof for those lessons. You shouldn't use the verse to prove that "Jesus is coming again" ("have eternal life"). Your proof would be too indirect.

Whenever you have to do much explaining to show that your proof fits your lesson, the proof is probably too indirect. Use a proof that's simpler, one that your people can catch quicker.

Rule 5. The illustration/application must directly fit the lesson. Some illustrations give the lesson only a glancing blow, or require a lot of explaining. You have to go all the way around the barn to make them fit. Save yourself and especially your audience the trip. The lesson and application must fit together like hand and glove if the application is to go on teaching the lesson when your listener leaves the church.

Rule 6. The illustration/application must practically apply the lesson to life. When your illustration is about an astronaut soaring into space you may need to take some time afterward to show how the illustration and lesson apply to contemporary life. But when you tell of the anticipation you feel while waiting for your dinner to cook, the application may be right in the story. Jesus illustrated with things people would often do so that the lesson of his sermon was repeated every time they did it.

Chapter 3

Ten Steps in Sermon Preparation

There is no one orthodox method of preparing a sermon. You'll find the best way for you only by trial and error. However, since the task can seem so overwhelming to the beginner, the remainder of this book will focus on one simplified approach—the Segment Method of sermon preparation. I urge you to try it precisely and rigidly at first to learn its significant advantages. Later, adapt it to fit your particular personality and gifts.

301. Step 1: Choose Your Bible Passage or Topic

Here are three questions that will help you choose your passage or topic:

1. What is your objective? Precisely what do you hope to have happen to your listeners as a result of hearing this sermon? All preachers should study their Bibles. But the best preachers will also study their people. What are their needs? Where are they hurting?

Some particular problem or need in the congregation may lead you to want to preach on a given subject. However, it must be a need faced by a large majority of the church family and not just one or two members. Your responsibility is to lead everyone in worship, not just a selected few. Besides, when you plan a sermon for a specific person, the devil is surprisingly often successful in keeping him/her out of church that day.

Our general objective is always the same, to help worshipers love Jesus more. But our specific objective varies. Is it to pray more? Give more? Read the Bible more? Spend time with the family more? You need a specific objective in mind before you begin.

2. What will be your sermon type? Expository? Topical? Biographical/ Narrative? Textual? (See Section 206.) Remember, it's not wrong to choose a subject before you go to the Bible. It is wrong to decide what you're going to say about it before going to the Bible. Unfortunately, this will likely be your temptation. Deciding what to say, then finding a Bible text that allows you to say it is not biblical preaching, but hypocritical preaching—the preaching of oneself while pretending to be preaching Scripture.

From here on we'll use the expository sermon as an example for the sake of simplicity. It is probably the easiest type to keep biblical. Incidentally, one of the simplest may be an expository sermon based on one of Jesus parables.

3. What have you recently read? Anytime you seem to have nothing to preach about, check honestly and you'll almost certainly find it's because you have not been thoughtfully studying your Bible on a daily basis. Choosing your passage can be one of the most frustrating and time consuming parts of sermon preparation if left to the moment it's needed. On the other hand, if you have been experientially studying the Word on a regular basis, you'll have more passages crying out to be preached than you'll ever find use for.

I would recommend again that you keep a journal when you read your Bible devotionally. It not only makes your devotions more meaningful, but will give a backlog of potential sermons. Look through your journal. What's inspired you once will probably inspire you again. And what's inspired you has the best chance of inspiring your listeners.

Or keep a "sermon garden," some place where you write down passages and ideas you'd like to preach someday. If all you write down is a possible text, good. If you add some thoughts you've gleaned from it or some illustrations that fit it, even better.

Henry Ward Beecher kept what he called a "drawer of apples." When texts or subjects came to him he wrote down some thoughts on them and put the notes in a drawer. When it came time to prepare a sermon he would go to his "drawer of apples" and find some of the ideas were still green and hard and some just beginning to color. But invariably some were mature and mellow, and one of these he would choose as he began his sermon preparation.

302. Step 2: Study Your Passage to Find Segment Lessons and Proofs

This is your biggest step. Of the ten steps, this step and the next will likely take more time than on all the other eight put together.

Do not sit down saying, "I'm going to think up some sermon segments." This would be wrong for at least two reasons: First, you would be giving your own ideas off the top of your head and they would tend to be shallow, mundane ideas your listeners may already have heard a hundred times. Second, all three parts of the sermon segment (lesson, proof, illustration/application) are not likely to come to you at once. *Begin by looking principally for lesson and proof.* (See Section 207-B.)

302-A. How to Study Your Passage
Start with your Bible. A speech becomes a sermon when it originates in

Scripture. Man's word about God is merely a speech. Only God's word about man is a sermon. True preaching is God's word to mankind rather than mankind's word about God. And since the Bible is the most inspired and accurate word we have from God, it must be primary in our preaching. Otherwise, our speeches aren't really sermons.

And always open your Bible with prayer, asking God to give you something He wants shared with His people. Only the Holy Spirit who gave the Scripture can interpret it to human hearts.

Read your passage rapidly several times, asking three questions: 1. What does it say (investigation)? 2. What does it mean (interpretation)? 3. What difference does it make (application)? Get the overview first and you'll make fewer mistakes interpreting the details later. See the forest as a whole before examining the trees and their leaves. What is the author talking about? Even more important, what is he saying about it?

Read your passage slowly, carefully, meditatively. Look for key words. Read it in every translation or version available—just be careful not to depend too heavily on ideas coming from paraphrases or dynamic versions. (See Section 204-A.)

What is the context? Knowing what is talked about before and after your passage will help you interpret your passage. If you have the time, a more complete study of context would include who wrote your passage, to whom and why.

What is the setting? Visualize the scene. Who are the principal persons in the passage and what does each stand for? Who is talking? To whom? Under what circumstances? What are the religious, political, and social settings?

Use the Bible simply. We must never be shallow, but we must always be clear. Don't overprove. You can kill a mosquito by dropping a bomb on it, but that's overdoing it. Many people in our congregations think the Bible is boring, and it's partially because we've taught them to believe it by the types of sermons we preach. In your study, sift through the ore minutely, intensively. In the pulpit, show only the nuggets.

Use the Bible honestly. In the process of sermon preparation, our ego is always at risk. The desire for creativity may so overwhelm us that, perceiving an original idea, we preach it even if we're not sure of it. Or we preach a possible interpretation as though it were certain. We alienate our intelligent listeners by preaching little half-lies in support of great truths. New is important. But true is imperative.

What does it teach about hope? People don't have to come to church to know they're sinners, but they may have to come to know there's hope. Negative sermons may stop wrong action, but they don't motivate to right action.

The dictionary definition of a sermon is "an annoying harangue." Shame on us. Accentuate the positive. That's the way Paul preached, ". . . We preached the gospel of God to you . . . encouraging, comforting and urging you to live lives worthy of God, who calls you into his kingdom and glory" (I Thess 2:9, 12).

People must know they are sinners before they will seek salvation. However, your first calling is not to denounce sin, but to announce salvation. The most successful preaching is invariably hope-centered preaching. Never send people home on flat tires. The word "gospel" means good news. If you're not preaching good news, you're not preaching the gospel!

What does it teach about Jesus? Ellen White counsels, "In your labor do not be dictatorial, do not be severe, do not be antagonistic. Preach the love of Christ, and this will melt and subdue hearts" (*Manuscript Releases*, vol. 3, p.34). We are the disciples of a person, devoted to a person, advocates for a person, and that person is Jesus Christ.

A sermon is like the spoke of a wheel. It must be fastened to Christ at one end and relate to life at the other. A spoke does no good, bears no weight unless fastened at both ends.

Christ-centered sermons draw. Jesus promised, "But I, when I am lifted up from the earth, will draw all men to myself" (John 12:32). Do you hope people will love your sermon? They'll invariably love anything or anyone that introduces them to Jesus.

What do Bible commentaries say about it? First, of course, we read the Bible. But second only to that should be Bible commentaries. They should not come until after we have gotten everything we can directly from the Bible. But they should probably come before we go anywhere else. They give us more biblical insights per minute of study time, and they help protect us from expository misinterpretations.

The divine commentaries of Ellen White should come first. Remember her counsel that the Bible should first be studied thoroughly, next go to her writings to see if there's something there that helps, then go into the pulpit and preach from the Bible. (See Section 204-C.)

Three good rules for using the Spirit of Prophecy in preaching: First, study your Bible before going to Ellen White, thus keeping the Bible predominate.

Second, use brief, pithy quotations. Don't quote a paragraph if a single sentence says what you really want to teach.

Third, use mostly positive statements from Mrs. White. Nobody learns to love whatever is used to spank them.

What do books other than the Bible say? Once you've exhausted your Bible passage, if you feel a need for more material, study what nonbiblical authors have written that expands what you've gotten from the Bible.

Use quotations judiciously. Here are a few guidelines for the use of quotations:

Quote to add authority. Use quotations if listeners would recognize the writer as an authority they would more readily accept than yourself.

Quote to say it better. If someone has coined a phrase that says precisely and memorably what you want to say, quote it.

Quote understandably. Don't quote too many statistics. Used sparingly, they can be dramatic. Used voluminously, they may be boring and hard to understand. Poetry can add an artistic touch to your sermon, but you must be sure you're using it because it's meaningful to your listeners and not just because you enjoy it. Most poetry was written to be read rather than spoken. It may be so deep that it needs to be studied and meditated on to be completely understood. You can do that as you read at home; your listeners cannot as they listen at church.

Quote honestly. You can be honest while borrowing a few ideas here and there without giving credit. But you cannot be honest if you borrow a significant number of words or the argument and organization of a chapter without crediting the author.

Honesty and accuracy necessitate careful note-taking as you study. Writing down a complete bibliographical reference is a nuisance, but if you're ever called to question or if you want to restudy the subject later, you'll be glad that you have all the information—including the library from which you got the book.

Quote briefly. Don't read whole pages in the pulpit. Don't read a whole paragraph if you're really after just one sentence. Don't read the whole sentence if a single phrase carries your thought. Certainly, you must avoid using quotations out of context. But the point is that if you are talking about lesson A, quote only what deals with A—even if it means you use only a portion of a sentence. Don't allow your quotations to encourage your listeners to wander off onto B, C, or D.

302-B. A Special Way to Take Notes

Use small (3-x5-inch) note paper for material. As you begin studying your Bible passage, have lots of small note paper available, perhaps about three by five inches. If necessary, make your own out of scrap paper. I would discourage your using cards. They're too expensive and too bulky for filing away as we'll suggest later. If you have a computer, use the columns setting so the printed copy can be cut up into some size approximating 3x5's.

The important thing is that every worthwhile thought you come across in your research of the Bible passage end up on a separate piece of paper. Later, when you begin to form your sermon segments you can merely shuffle these pieces of paper around until the right idea, proof and illustration/application come together. In other words, if you take your notes on several large pieces of paper, you may later decide that a lesson and proof on page one fits an illustration\application on page four. It's much simpler and a real time saver to have them on separate pieces of paper so you can lay them together and have your sermon segment without a lot of recopying, scratching out, etc.

Write down every lesson and proof you might conceivably use—even if they're not too great. A further idea may come along later to enlarge it and make it usable. (See Section 207-D for rules of good segment lessons and proofs.)

Be aware that you'll eventually need an illustration/application to go with each lesson and proof, but don't worry too much about it at this point. Pause as each lesson comes and prayerfully ask the Lord to show you life situations to help illustrate or apply it. But be patient. The Lord doesn't always answer prayers immediately.

Use large (8 ½- x 11-inch) note paper for organization. At the top of a large sheet of paper, perhaps about eight and one-half by eleven inches, write "Possible outline." In the middle of the sheet write "Possible theme." Here's why:

Develop your outline as you go. As you study and pray, the love relationship between you and your Lord seems about to produce something beautiful. Then disaster strikes. The inspirational ideas are there, but you don't seem able to organize them into a logical, coherent sermon. You feel so strongly that you have found something important to say, but you just can't organize it into a rational way of saying it. The sermon dies before it's born—sermonic miscarriage.

That need never happen. Here are three "don'ts" and one "do" that will prevent the disaster of sermonic miscarriage.

Don't preach without organizing. Many dread sermon organization because it's probably the hardest mental work the preacher does. It requires more mental discipline than does the biblical research. Which ideas are more valuable than others? Which are related to one another? Which should precede the other? But it's worth the work. Good organization makes a sermon easier to preach, easier to listen to, and easier to understand.

Don't organize before you research. Preachers sometimes take great pride in having their outline before they begin their study, or even in finding someone else's outline on which to build their sermon. But what if your research fails to turn up the right material? You can only preach ideas you find. If what you find doesn't fit your preconceived outline—sermonic miscarriage.

Don't organize after you research. Some enjoy Bible study and looking for sermon lessons, but rather dread organizing them. Their tendency is to seek out lots of material, then, at the last minute, try to find an outline under which to organize it. It's a frightfully frustrating experience. The ideas are so intermingled and there are so many. You just can't make sense out of all that wad of material—sermonic miscarriage.

Do organize as you research. Every time you write an idea on a 3x5 ask yourself, "Could this be a point on my outline? Or does it suggest a possible skeleton for organizing my sermon?" If the answer is no, don't worry about it. If the answer is yes, scribble it down on your large sheet under "Possible Outlines."

302-C. Develop Your Theme as You Go

The sermon theme is the gist of the sermon in one sentence. You need to differentiate between the three "t's" of preaching: Your **topic** is your general subject. Your *title* is what you call it. Your *theme* is what you're going to say about it.

It's not too helpful for listeners to go away remembering your subject. It is helpful if they remember your theme. You don't want them saying you talked about the sanctuary, but a specific lesson the sanctuary teaches, such as, "We are saved, not because we're good, but because Christ is good." You don't want people going away saying you talked about the church, but something special about the church such as, "The church is a place where, surrounded by loving Christians, we learn to love Christ."

The theme is not some formal homiletic requirement to get in the way of opening yourself to your people. Ask yourself what your heart burden is, what you specifically want the people to take out the door with them. Then put it in a brief, memorable sentence and you have your theme. You may well find this the hardest and most exacting, yet the most fruitful part of sermon preparation.

Your theme helps you and your congregation know the purpose of your sermon. As the story goes, a white-haired couple sat in the front row of church. But he was awfully hard of hearing. As the preacher preached, the old man turned to his wife and, in a hoarse whisper, asked, "What's he talking about?" She listened a little longer, shook her head, then leaned over and answered loud enough for him and half the church to hear, "He don't say." A theme prevents you from talking without you or the congregation knowing what you're talking about.

Your theme helps your sermon make a deeper impression. The best sermons do not tax listeners by saying a great many things, but inspire them by saying one thing in a great many ways. That one thing is your theme. Make everything else in your sermon focus on and amplify it, and it will go out the door with your congregation.

Ellen White described ineffective preachers, "They touched here and there, bringing a large mass of matter which they regarded as convincing and overwhelming evidence, but in fact they buried the truth under a mass of matter poured out upon the hearers, so that the points never could be found. Everything they presented was muddled. So many subjects were brought into one discourse that no point stood proved and clear" (*Letter* 47, 1886).

At the beach, you lie comfortably in the warm sun just about to fall asleep. But a boy with a magnifying glass focuses that same soothing sun on one spot in your back and suddenly you're wide awake. Preach a little of this, a little of that and a bit of something else and your congregation may be comfortably lulled to sleep. But focus on one Bible-based, Christ-centered theme and you'll wake your people up.

Whenever you put an idea on a 3x5 ask yourself if this could become your theme. If not, don't worry about it at this juncture. But if so, scratch it down on your large sheet of paper under "Possible Themes."

A sermon is like a river with tributaries running into it. The river is the sermon theme and the tributaries are the various parts of your sermon outline. Just as each tributary flows into and expands a river, each part of your outline flows into and expands the sermon theme. But the flow of water begins in the tributaries before it flows in the river. That is, you can't settle on your theme until you know what material you have to pour into it. Your theme must grow out of your research material. Ideally, it should come to you, neither before you study nor after you study, but as you study.

303. Step 3: Add Illustrations/Applications to Complete Your Segments

In Step Two, you were taught to prepare lots of lessons and proofs. Now it's time to add the third and last part to each sermon segment, your illustration/application. Lesson and proof will almost certainly come whenever you prayerfully apply yourself to the seat of your chair and your eyes to a page of your Bible. Illustrations/applications, on the other hand, may come best as you go about your normal business with lesson and proof in the back of your mind.

Whenever you have the lesson and proof but can't come up with the illustration/application it's probably for one of two reasons. One, your lesson is not practical enough, not closely enough related to life. Or two, you have not had the lesson in mind long enough to have taken it with you into enough life situations.

Purposely keep lesson and proof simmering in the back of your brain as you do other things. This will both provide a beautiful spiritual experience for you and will help you come up with contemporary applications. Carry paper. Write it down. Forget that you can remember and remember that you can forget. They claim one fellow moving along through his daily routine suddenly got such a beautiful idea for his sermon that he immediately knelt to thank God for it. But when he got up, he'd forgotten what it was! Write it down.

303-A. Importance of Practical Application
Practical application answers the question, "So what?" "What does this mean to me?" "What difference will it make in my everyday life?" To make a Bible lesson or principle come alive, give specific real-life examples of how someone faced this issue and how he or she handled it.

One parishioner complained, "Our preacher is always scratching us where we don't itch." By nature we're mostly interested in ourselves. I get excited showing photographs of my family, where I've been, what I've done. But these same pictures that excite me bore everybody else, because they're not in the picture. Truth moves from boring to exciting when it puts your people into the picture by showing how it applies to their families, where they've been, what they've done. People's first interest is themselves. Make your sermon about them and they'll be interested in your sermon.

Practical application is especially important right now because it's especially important to young people. The grandparents in your audience are from the "Old Timers" generation which asks, "Is it true?" Preachers can reach them by proving their points. But that generation didn't talk enough about love and so the parents in your congregation are from the "Baby Boomer" generation which asks, "Is it loving?" You can reach them by talking love and relationship. But that generation has produced more broken homes than ever and so the youth in the church are from the "Baby Buster" generation which asks, "Will it work?" They want practical application.

Practical application must be very important to God, because His Word is so full of it. Most of the Old Testament is not theological theory, but the story of God's attempting to lead His people through the practical problems of everyday living. Most of Paul's writing was as a pastor addressing himself to his people's specific needs and temptations. Most of Jesus' teaching was in parable form so that people could understand truth as it related to life.

When Jesus' disciples came to the temple they said, "Look, what magnificent buildings." When Jesus came to the temple He said, "Look at that widow giving her offering." The disciples saw things, but Jesus saw people. God's first love is not ideas, but people. Truth is meaningful only if it helps people.

A circle rotates around one central point. An ellipse rotates around two. Every sermon should be elliptical. It focuses on two centers, not one. Not just Bible truth. Not just human need. Always on both.

The most successful sermon is that which matches an understanding of religion in the abstract with a knowledge of human nature in the concrete. Your entire sermon must not come from books, not even the Book. You must know something about Bible characters, but even more about the character of your own congregation. You need to know something about the city of Jerusalem, but even more about the city where your people work and worship.

A word of warning, though. Be aware of people's sociological and psychological needs, but beware of going into the pulpit sounding like a sociologist or psychologist. People's practical needs are best met by their becoming aware of and being saved from their sins through Jesus Christ. To preach the gospel is not to neglect human problems, but to offer divine answers to those problems.

303-B. Importance of Illustrations
Illustrations were emphasized in Jesus' preaching. Illustrations are

especially important to Christian preachers because they were so important to Christ's preaching. "He did not say anything to them without using a parable" (Mark 4:34). With Jesus, the kingdom was always "like" something. (See Matthew 13:24, 33, 44, 45, 47.) Ellen White begins her book, *Christ's Object Lessons*, "In Christ's parable teaching the same principle is seen as in His own mission to the world. . . . God was made manifest in the likeness of men. So it was in Christ's teaching: *the unknown was illustrated by the known;* divine truths by earthly things with which the people were most familiar" (p. 17).

Illustrations help hold attention. Never forget, it's not the amount of truth you *give* that counts, but the amount your listeners *receive*. Romans 10:17 contains a formula for faith, "So then faith comes by hearing, and hearing by the word of God" (NKJV). The formula: Word + hearing = faith. That part of what you preach that people do not hear, no matter how biblical, cannot build their faith. Only what gets their attention determines their action. We do not seek people's attention so we can entertain them, but we must seek it before we can teach them.

It's a somewhat judgmental theory, but some say that little minds dwell on people, mediocre minds dwell on things, and large minds dwell on ideas. Then how did Jesus get truth into little and mediocre minds? By associating them with people and things.

Illustrations motivate by adding emotion to your logic. The Adventist preacher instinctively fears overly emotional preaching, and rightly so. But we must never shun it entirely, for people usually do only the things they feel like doing. They can believe through logic alone, but they'll likely act on that belief according to how they feel about it. Worshipers do not come to church so much to learn what they never knew as to be motivated to do what they already knew they should.

Imagine that I want to go sailing but can't afford both a rudder and a sail for the boat I've rented. Deciding in favor of the rudder, I install it and push off from the dock with the rudder in total control of the boat, but going absolutely nowhere. I trade the rudder for a sail. Now the wind pushes me across the lake faster and faster until, totally out of control, I crash into the other side. Which do you need to sail a boat, a rudder or a sail? Both. The rudder represents logic, the sail emotion. Which do you need to preach effectively? Both.

Illustrations help listeners retain truth longer. A sermon lesson is like a nail. An illustration is like a hammer that drives the nail home. If you want your sermon to go on preaching itself all week long, do as Jesus did. Illustrate it with things people will be doing all week long.

Thus far we've talked about illustration and application separately. However, since the typical and ideal practical application comes from an illustration that applies your segment lesson to life, we will now, for the sake of brevity, refer to illustration/application as illustration.

303-C. How to Use Illustrations

The reason we use an illustration is to make the lesson easier to understand and show how it applies to life. A storytelling preacher tells a story to entertain, an illustrating preacher uses it to teach and apply a spiritual lesson. In other words, if you don't have a lesson to illustrate don't illustrate it.

The word "illustrate" comes from the Latin "lux" meaning light. A light is of no value unless it has something on which to shine. Point your flashlight at the sky and it does no good. Point it at a picture of Jesus and it helps you see Him more clearly. Use illustrations to shine light on your lessons. Illustrations must always be incidental to your sermon. They are not themselves the sermon.

Illustrations should almost never be read, even if the rest of your sermon is. As you prepare, see the illustration as though you were living it. If you see it, it's much easier to tell it in a way that will help your audience see it.

Tell it always with your lesson in mind. Accentuate the parts of your story that teach your lesson and abbreviate any part that doesn't. Remember, a story is well told only if your listener remembers the lesson.

303-D. Humorous Illustrations

Humor must never be used just to entertain. Preachers may be unconsciously tempted to do this because it's too often the only time they get any positive response from the audience. But Ellen White reminds us that preaching is serious business and must never be approached frivolously. A good sense of humor is a sign of a healthy mind, but use humor only incidentally and only if it teaches the spiritual lessons God has laid on your heart.

303-E. Sources of Illustrations

Use Bible illustrations. Bible illustrations have the advantage of carrying the authority of Scripture. Unfortunately, using the same Bible stories in the same way your listener has already heard them a hundred times doesn't hold attention well. Use the less familiar stories. Or research stories so they come alive and are seen in a new light. Or contemporize, by putting them in a modern setting.

Cultivate a homiletic bias. That is, look for sermon illustrations everywhere you go and in everything you see. When you can't find an illustration it's not usually because it's not available, but because you haven't developed the habit of seeing the world in moral colors. Homiletic bias means keeping our minds focused on finding divine lessons in human experiences. Thus it is actually a form of "praying without ceasing."

Besides the Bible, take illustrations from other good literature, biographies, science, sports, art, newspapers, magazines, history, family life, congregational life. Study anything that helps you understand human nature.

There is no better way to find illustrations than to start your sermon early in the week so you know what lessons you want to teach. Then, develop your homiletic bias by looking for ways to illustrate those lessons through things you experience or pull out of your memory throughout the week.

Use past experiences. Jesus said, "You will be my witnesses" (Acts 1:8). Too many of us want to be lawyers arguing the fine points of the law. A witness is one who has had a personal experience and shares it with others. Preaching is not only the proclamation of a truth, it is also the sharing of an experience.

An illustration can be anything out of your past that teaches a spiritual lesson, but preferably your experience with the truth being taught. How has this problem been your problem? How has this truth helped you, solved your problem?

By all means, use personal illustrations. An expert should be able to compose a biography of your life after hearing you preach over an extended period of time. But remember, people are listening between the lines to find out what kind of person you really are. Don't give away confidences. Don't belittle your spouse or children. Don't be the hero of every story as though you always handled every situation perfectly. Other people know they don't and if you seem to think you do, they may question both your humility and your integrity.

Use imagination. Jesus surely exercised imagination in using such illustrations as the story of the Rich Man and Lazarus. But always use imagination honestly. Don't pretend you're telling a true story if you aren't. Introduce your imaginary story with a prefix such as "Imagine with me." Or, "Let's pretend." Or, "What if."

Use books of illustrations if you have access to them. But use them mostly as "pump primers" to remind you of some personal past experience that illustrates your lesson. Your own is better even if it's not so good, because it comes out of the warmth of your own heart.

303-F. Fill Out Your Segments

Now you've finished gathering your material. Hopefully, everything you're going to say is on your 3x5's. Remember the three parts of a segment are lesson, proof and illustration/application. If your lessons came as you studied your Bible, chances are you already have lesson and proof on the same 3x5. But your illustration will likely be separate. Your next task is to find the best illustration or application to fit each lesson, thus filling out your segments. The time-saving advantage of the 3x5's is that you don't have to do any recopying. Simply lay together on your desk or table the 3x5's that make up each segment. Seldom use more than one illustration per segment. The illustration's purpose is to clarify and apply. When you preach, if one illustration will do that, move on to the next lesson. It's the lessons we're after, not the stories.

304. Step 4: Choose Theme and Outline

If you've followed the suggestion made in Step 2 (see Section 302-B) above, you now have an 8 $\frac{1}{2}$- x 11-inch sheet of paper, with the top half all scratched up with possible themes and the lower half with possible sermon outlines. Now is the time you'll be most thankful you did it, for you now have several possible themes and outlines from which to choose.

304-A. Choose Your Theme

A theme is the gist of your whole sermon in a sentence. (See Section 302-C.) It is the one idea you most want people to take home. Your theme must be **true**, that is, Biblical. It must be *important*, a big idea worth your listener's time. It must be *interesting*, fresh, contemporary, practical. It must lead to **Christ**. We should never forget that, in one sense, every sermon should have but one theme—Christ. In choosing your theme, always ask yourself, "How does this theme, how will this sermon uplift Jesus Christ?"

The theme must fit your material. No matter how good a theme might be nor how much you'd like to use it, save it for another sermon if it doesn't fit a significant number of your segments. You can't preach on something until you've found plenty to say about it. Hopefully, if you used the large sheet to scratch down possible themes as you gathered your material, your theme and your material are closely related.

A theme should be worded properly. Let's say a good theme would be: **Christians look at ultimate, not just immediate rewards.** Below are five rules for wording a theme, followed by five variations on the above theme that break these rules. A theme should be:

A point of view, not just a subject. Wrong: A comparison between looking at ultimate and immediate rewards.

Simple, not complicated. Wrong: Spiritual productivity necessitates eventual goals precluding instant.

Declarative, not interrogative. Wrong: Do Christians look at ultimate, or just immediate rewards?

Straightforward, not an analogy. Wrong: Christian eyesight focuses on overcoming shortsightedness.

Positive, not negative. Wrong: Christians do not look at just immediate rewards.

304-B. Choose Your Outline

Now that you have your theme you're ready to choose the outline. With the help of the outline ideas from your 8½- x 11 sheet, choose an outline that best uses your segments to teach your theme.

304-C. Sample Themes and Outlines

Here are three samples of themes and the sermon outlines that teach and enlarge on them.

First, a topical sermon on the Sabbath:

Theme: *Love demands time together*

    I. On Sabbath, through worship, we learn of God's love

    II. On Sabbath, through nature, we see God's love

    III. On Sabbath, through family togetherness, we experience God's love

    IV. On Sabbath, through missionary activity, we share God's love

Second, a more detailed outline of an expository sermon from John 4:

Theme: *To be Christlike is to be a soulwinner*

    I. To be Christlike is to go out of our way for the sake of others. [A segment based on verses 3, 4]

    II. To be Christlike is to work even when weary

        A. Physical needs get too much of our time. [Segment based on vs. 8]

        B. Meeting Jesus makes physical things seem less important. [Segment based on vs. 28-30]

    III. To be Christlike is to value the single soul. [Segment based on vs. 7a]

    IV. To be Christlike is to win others through kindness

        A. Kindness attracts. [Segment based on vs. 7]

        B. Kindness reaching down the social ladder is most effective. [Segment based on vs. 9]

    V. To be Christlike is to be an excitable soulwinner. [Segment based on vs. 31-34]

(See Section 515 for a complete outline.)

Third, a detailed outline of an expository sermon from Psalm 46:

Theme: *Nothing can destroy what's in God's hands*

    I. Christian calm amidst calamity when God present

        A. Not promise prevent trouble, but be present when trouble comes. [Segment based on vs. 1]

        B. Every physical (human) refuge eventually fails. [Segment based on vs. 2, 3]

    II. The church is invincible when God is present

        A. God is in His church. [Segment based on vs. 4]

        B. God is in His church at every level. [Segment based on vs. 4a]

        C. Church's temptation, keep God nearby rather than within. [Segment based on vs. 5a]

        D. Only God's presence makes church invincible.[Segment based on vs. 5b]

    III. Practice God's presence in both good times and bad

        A. When things go right take time to look for God. [Segment based on vs. 8, 9]

        B. It takes time to ponder God's goodness. [Segment based on vs. 10]

C. When things go wrong remember that what He's done before He
   can do again. [Segment based on vs. 11]
(See Section 502 for a complete sermon based on this outline.)

305. Step 5: Organize Your Sermon

We've researched our Bible and brought out the lessons and proofs we feel
the Holy Spirit wants us to share with our people. We have made segments by
matching these lessons and proofs with illustrations. We have settled on our
theme and know we have many segments that fit it. Thus, we've already made
a good beginning at organizing our sermon.

However, some find sermon organization such grueling work they're
tempted to neglect it and just get up and talk. This is like having a stack of
building materials we hope to make into a house without having a houseplan.
We've talked a little about organization, but we need to emphasize now why
it's so important.

305-A. Purpose of Organization

Bones tend to repel rather than attract. We use skeletons to frighten people.
Yet put skin and muscles on them, and we find them beautiful. In fact, without
bones, the skin and muscles of the perfectly proportioned athlete and the
beautiful woman would fall to the floor, a useless, unattractive blob. Skeletons
aren't beautiful, but there's no human beauty without them.

In preaching we call the sermon outline or organization the skeleton. On
this skeleton we hang the muscle of our biblical evidence, logical arguments,
and practical application. Then we add the skin of our delivery and call it a
sermon.

Sometimes we're tempted to treat the content and delivery as important
while regarding the sermon skeleton or outline as unimportant and even
unnecessary. We must remember that muscle and skin are of little value without
bones.

Good organization makes a sermon easier to preach. It forces us to be more
logical, to determine which idea is the tree, which is a branch of the tree, and
which is a branch of a branch. By using a simple, easy-to-remember outline,
you can almost preach a sermon without notes. And what's easy for you to
remember will always be easier for your listeners to remember.

Good organization makes a sermon easier to listen to. The difference
between a five-course meal and hash is organization. Diners prefer to be served
appetizer, soup, salad, entree and dessert separately and in the proper order.
If the cook were to mix together the ingredients that make up all five of these
courses and serve them as hash, the diners would complain. People want their
meals and their sermons organized.

Human nature instinctively desires order. In fact, listening to a disorganized sermon may so frustrate the housekeeper who has a precise place for everything in her kitchen and the man who keeps his tools in a certain order on his workbench, that they miss the message and lose the blessing.

Good organization makes a sermon easier to understand. Notice the chapters of a book or the articles in a magazine. Almost invariably, subtitles divide and simplify the content. If writers show their skeletons to make their work more understandable, it is doubly important that speakers do so. Readers can go back and reread what they have missed or misunderstood. Listeners cannot.

Shun the shallow, but embrace the simple. The less experienced we are in preaching, the more fearful we are that being simple will make our sermon simplistic. Actually, we're much more likely to be talking over the heads of our listeners. If you've something significant to say, organizing it in a simple way doesn't make it simplistic—just understandable.

Any simpleton can make easy things difficult to understand. Genius is making difficult things easy to understand. Be like the coal miner who digs deep into the earth to find coal. But he doesn't go to the surface and put up a sign saying, "There's coal down there and if you could dig as I've dug you'd find it." No, miners aren't done when they find the coal. They must bring it to the surface and make it available to every hearth. Preachers aren't done when they find truth. They must bring it to the surface—organize it to be understandable and available to every heart.

Be more concerned about making your outline clear than clever. Clever is good, but clear is essential. Your goal should always be to bring your listeners *deep thoughts—simply expressed—*and *practically applied.*

A sermon has three parts: introduction, body and conclusion. Basically, you have three tasks in preaching—to interest, to instruct and to impress or lead to decision. Interest is emphasized in the introduction, instruction in the body, and impression or decision in the conclusion.

305-B. Introduction

The introduction is the first part of the sermon presented, but it should be one of the last parts of the sermon prepared. It's important to know something about persons before you introduce them to others. And it's necessary to know a great deal about your sermon before you decide how to introduce it to your audience.

The introduction should not likely comprise more than 10 to 15 percent of your sermon. Don't spend so much time setting the table that there's too little time left for the meal.

Here are three basic purposes of the introduction:

The introduction gains attention. During the first two to three minutes of your sermon you have the unsolicited attention of your congregation. Their good intentions and mere curiosity have them wondering what you'll do, what you'll say. After that, you get only what you earn.

Never stand up until you know exactly what the first and last sentence of your sermon will be. Make that first pitch right across the plate, belt-high. If you don't get your listeners' attention in the first 60 seconds, you may never get it. Or, as one speaker put it, "If you don't strike oil in the first minute, stop boring!"

Your purpose is not only to gain your listener's interest, but to gain their interest in your topic. I heard a minister whose topic was legalistic religion begin "Nineteen hundred years ago there was a religious group who kept all the Ten Commandments, paid a faithful tithe, was most faithful in every detail of religious life—and they murdered Christ!" Now there's an introduction that aroused interest in the topic.

How do you gain attention? Use an illustration such as the one above. Or ask a question. Start where your people are. Talk about a common problem and lead up to your sermon theme, which is your proposed answer to the problem.

The introduction gives your theme. Most speakers give their subject in the introduction, but few clarify their theme. The subject is much less interesting than a good theme, for the subject merely says what you're going to talk about. The theme tells what you're going to say about it. It is your sermon in a sentence. Don't say "I'm going to talk about attitudes." Rather, say "The thought I would like us to think through together this morning is this: We see things, not as they are, but as we are."

We sometimes speak of deductive versus inductive preaching or reasoning. Deductive logic reasons from the general to the specific. For example: Fido is a dog, all dogs have fleas. Therefore, Fido has fleas. Inductive logic reasons from the specific to the general: Fido scratches a lot, has bald spots on his coat and there are little black things crawling on him. Therefore, Fido has fleas.

Both deductive and inductive preaching are perfectly proper. Deductive preaching would put the theme in the introduction then proceed to prove the validity of it. Inductive preaching would lay out the evidence and illustrations for the audience to think through and come to the theme along with the preacher near the end of the sermon.

For the sake of clarity, I recommend a third alternative which is really a combination of the two. Give your theme in the introduction. Give it again in your conclusion. And give it anyplace in between where it fits, possibly at the beginning or close of at least some of your segments. Used repeatedly, your theme has the best chance of going out the door with your people.

Some don't want to give their theme in the introduction because they want to maintain an air of expectancy. But a good theme can awaken interest and make the rest of your sermon easier for listeners to understand. Remember, clever is good, but clear is essential.

The introduction can give a pre-summary. If you've seen the whole picture, a jigsaw puzzle is a lot easier to put together. If your introduction gives a little overview of your sermon, probably right after you give the theme, the congregation will find the sermon a lot easier to put together as they listen.

For example, you might tell them, "First we'll talk about *why* we ought to love; then we'll talk about *how* to love." The numbered outline is the very easiest to follow, "We'll find there are just three steps to heaven." Then each main division of your outline becomes one of the steps.

I wouldn't suggest that every sermon needs a pre-summary. But fear only simplistic ideas, not simple organization. You can't hit people between the eyes while you're preaching over their heads.

Sample introductions can be seen in the sermons at the back of this book:

Section 502's sermon begins with a problem to get attention on the topic, leading to the theme, leading to a pre-summary.

Section 503's sermon begins with an illustration and question to get attention on the topic, leading to a pre-summary, leading to the theme, leading to an illustration to help clarify the theme.

Section 504's sermon begins with a practical problem to get attention on the topic, leading to a Christ-centered theme and a little clarification of it. There is no pre-summary.

Section 505's sermon begins with an illustration to get attention, leading to a problem, leading to the theme. There's no pre-summary.

305-C. Body

The main portion of your sermon is called the sermon body. The sermon body is made up of your segments. That is, the basic lessons, proofs and illustrations/applications of the sermon. We won't spend more time with it here because it's what we worked on in steps one to four.

305-D. Conclusion

Preachers preach too many elephant sermons. An elephant sermon is one having a big head at the beginning, plenty of body in the middle, but almost no tail at the end! The conclusion seems just an afterthought. The Greeks, who probably organized effective speaking more precisely than any other culture, knew better. They called the conclusion the final struggle which decides the conflict.

Preaching a sermon is like flying an airplane. Some parts of it are fairly easy. But there are two crucial moments—getting off the ground, and especially landing the thing. Or, a sermon is like a love affair—it's easier to start one than to end one.

The conclusion is usually the hardest part of the sermon to prepare. However, it is also the most important part of the sermon. The lawyer knows that no matter how eloquently he argues his case, if his closing arguments don't draw forth a positive verdict, he fails. The salesman is well aware that no matter how fluent his sales presentation, if he doesn't know how to "close" so as to make a sale, he starves.

Preachers must learn the same lesson. It's important that the sermon introduction grasp the congregation's attention. It's important that the sermon body bring instruction and inspiration. But it's even more important that the sermon conclusion help listeners decide what action they're going to take. We must "close" for Christ; we must concentrate on the verdict.

This most important part of the sermon is also the most neglected. Maybe it's because we tend to run out of preparation time. Or perhaps we expect the heat of the moment to create the conclusion as we preach it. It is true that the Holy Spirit may cause us to *change* the conclusion somewhat as we preach, but I doubt that He often leads us to *prepare* it as we preach. The Spirit seldom overrides indolence.

The first part of the conclusion should be a *summary* of the sermon. The last part ought to be a *call to action*.

Summary. If the basic sermon theme and segments have been thought-provoking, repeating them constitutes a fair summary. But the ideal summary presents the sermon's basic thoughts in a new way. The congregation gets bored if we re-preach the sermon in the summary. The most interesting summary is a detailed example that illustrates the sermon's emphasis. Jesus concluded His Sermon on the Mount by using an illustration—of two houses, one built on rock and the other on sand.

Don't present any new arguments in the conclusion. To do so is to go contrary to its purpose, which is to recapitulate and apply the arguments or ideas already given. Thus, you will generally need only a few sentences in the summary portion of the conclusion.

Solomon didn't have preaching directly in mind, but he gave excellent preaching advice when he said, "Let us hear the conclusion of the **whole** matter" (Eccl.12:13, KJV). Too many conclusions unintentionally summarize only the last portion of the sermon body. You can drive your point deeper home if your summary pulls together your whole sermon.

Let's liken the sermon to a landscape painting and each division of the sermon body to an object in the painting—the tree, the cloud, the road, the horizon. When you stand up to preach, you have the entire picture in mind. You begin, in word pictures, to paint it for your congregation. To you the picture seems so clear, so simple. Surely everybody must see it. But many don't. You are most fortunate if the majority see the separate parts—the tree, cloud, road and horizon. In your summary, often for the first time, worshipers see how the individual parts of the sermon fit together. Only as you summarize do they see the full picture. And that's why a well-prepared summary is so essential!

Call to action. The sermon summary reviews and informs. The call to action challenges each listener to act on that information. The summary instructs the mind. The call to action confronts the will. A discourse is not really a sermon at all unless it does both.

Peter's sermon at Pentecost was one of the most successful sermons of all time. Its climax models well the ideal call to action: "Now when they heard this they were *cut to the heart,* and said to Peter and the rest of the apostles, 'Brethren, *what shall we do?'* And Peter said to them, 'Repent, and be baptized'" (Acts 2:37, 38, RSV).

A sermon should do more than dish out pleasant platitudes or helpful information. It should "cut to the heart" and leave listeners asking, "What shall we do?"

You've been in a home when there was a knock at the door. A voice from the kitchen announces, "There's somebody at the door." But the story doesn't end there. Things can never go back to normal until someone gets up and answers the door. A knock is not meant just to be announced, but to be answered. It demands action.

By means of their sermons, preachers intend to help listeners hear Jesus knocking at their doors. But proving He's there, available, is no way to end a sermon. A knock is not meant just to be announced. It is meant to be answered. It demands action. Every sermon should include a logical, nonmanipulative call to action. It can come in the form of a question asked, options suggested, or a challenge offered.

The ideal call to action invites the listeners to experience here and now what the sermon has just taught. You don't preach on forgiveness so that people will believe in forgiveness, but so that by believing, they will experience forgiveness—now.

Final words. Charles Reynolds Brown likened preachers who haven't prepared the final words of their sermons to a helpless crow, flying back and forth above a picket fence of sharpened stakes, looking in vain for a place to land. We've all suffered along with speakers who were feeling like that poor crow. They wanted to come down but didn't know where to land.

Landing options are almost endless: state what change you hope the sermon will make to the individual, restate your theme, read a text, use a portion of the closing hymn, give a poem, repeat your title, offer a prayer, ask for some physical response such raising a hand, standing, or coming forward. The possible plans for an ending are almost unlimited. But do plan. Don't ever stand up until you have some plan for how you're going to get sat down.

History suggests that on occasion, Magellan the explorer, sailed on and on into the unknown while people aboard his ship prayed for land. Never preach a Magellan sermon, sailing on and on while your people pray for land. In the introduction of your sermon tell them what you're going to tell them. In the body, tell them. In the conclusion, tell them what you've told them and what they should do about it—and sit down!

Sample conclusions can be seen in the sermons at the back of this book:

Section 504's sermon conclusion begins with a summary that is a repeat of the two main divisions, leading to an illustration, leading to an appeal for action.

Section 505's sermon conclusion begins with a summary that repeats the theme, leading to an illustration, leading to an appeal for decision.

Section 506's sermon conclusion begins with a summary that repeats the main divisions, leading to practical application, leading to an appeal, leading to the theme as the closing words.

Section 507's sermon conclusion begins with a summary that repeats the theme and re-worded main divisions and the subdivisions of the last division, leading to an illustration, leading to an appeal.

305-E. Lay Out 3X5'S

You've settled on what you expect at this point your outline will be. Now put each part of that outline on a separate 3x5 and lay these out in order on the far side of your desk or table. I like to write in red, designating these 3x5's as the sermon outline. If you were preparing the sermon under Section 502 of this book, the 3x5 on your far left would say "Introduction". To the right of it would be a 3x5 saying "Christian Calm Amidst Calamity When God Present." To the right of that "Not promise prevent trouble, but be present when trouble comes." To the right of that "Every physical (human) refuge eventually fails," etc. The last 3x5 on your far right would say "Conclusion." In other words, as you read across from left to right on the far side of your table or desk, you will be reading the outline of your sermon.

Now start through the segments you've already prepared, placing each under the part of the outline where it fits. When all your segment 3x5's are laid out, your sermon is virtually prepared before you.

306. Step 6: Change and Delete

It's a relief to have your outline prepared and your sermon laid out. If you had to, you could preach from what you now have. However, it's not necessary to follow your present plan inflexibly. It's now time to improve what you have by changing and deleting.

306-A. Change Outline

Some of your segments may not work with this outline. Either change the outline or put these segments away for use in another sermon. Look for balance in your outline. For example, if you have three divisions, but 80 percent of your material fits only one of the three, you should change the outline or the material you choose to keep. You may even need to change your theme to fit both material and outline.

306-B. Control Length

Before we talk about deleting material, we must emphasize the importance of controlling sermon length.

How long should a sermon be? It's an impossible question to answer for it depends on both the gifts of the speaker and the condition of the audience. Length must always fit the occasion. People don't listen well after the anticipated time to close. If you might begin late, have a plan for shortening your sermon. If yours is an afternoon or evening meeting, especially when people may have already been sitting several hours during the day, keep it short. If people are uncomfortable—too hot, too cold, too tired, can't hear without straining, in uncomfortable seats—keep it short. For most beginners in most situations, 20 to 25 minutes is probably a good rule of thumb.

It is practically impossible to end a long sermon with an effective conclusion and action step. By the time the preacher reaches the climax of such a sermon—when it's time to "take the order," or get the decision—people have quit listening.

Whatever portion of the sermon makes it too long detracts from the effectiveness of what went before. There is a listening curve. Benefit builds until the sermon gets to the top of that curve. Then benefit begins to fall. We can actually preach until worshipers go away from church worse off than when they came—even angry.

The final rule in sermon length must always be, *Stop while your listeners wish there were more, rather than after they wish there had been less.* Stop preaching before your people stop listening.

306-C. Delete Material

Poor preachers quit digging before they get enough material. Fair preachers quit when they have barely enough. The best preachers quit when they have twice as much as they'll need so they can enjoy the luxury of culling out everything but the very best. In deleting however, make it a habit to give preference to whatever relates most directly to Christ. He is always our central focus.

You'll learn to rely on your 3x5's to control sermon length. Experience will teach you that a certain number of 3x5's will produce a sermon of a given length. For me, each 3x5 will average about one minute of sermon—30 3x5's produce a 30 minute message.

Later, the 3x5's you keep can be filed away and your entire original research notes will be immediately available if you choose to use the sermon again. The 3x5's that are good material, but out of place in this sermon, should be filed away for future use.

The temptation to cheat as we prepare is almost overwhelming. "This is too important to leave out. Besides, it won't take long." And so we put things in, knowing full well we shouldn't. Deleting is difficult, especially if the ideas are our own. Besides, it's hard mental work deciding which is an A idea and which is a B. The best preachers are ruthless in preparation, putting a knife to the sermon's throat, eliminating every excess idea.

307. Step 7: Write Out Your Notes or Manuscript

Remember the three "T's?" First we choose the *topic*, what we're going to talk about. Then we choose the *theme*, what we're going to say about it. Finally, we choose the *title*, what we're going to call it. Before you write out whatever you're going to take into the pulpit, now is the time to choose your title.

307-A. Notes Versus Manuscript

What should you preach from? Manuscript? Notes? Nothing?

We usually think of four options: (1) *impromptu*—no specific preparation; (2) *extemporaneous*—thoughts prepared; (3) *manuscript*—thoughts and words prepared; (4) *memoriter*—thoughts and words prepared and memorized. Since numbers one and four are the extremes and seldom used by beginning preachers, we'll concentrate on the other two methods. Let's look at the advantages and disadvantages of extemporaneous preaching from notes versus manuscript preaching:

Preparation. In most cases manuscript preaching forces you to a more complete and precise preparation. Those who have written their sermons out can more exactly analyze them before delivering them.

Since those who preach from notes do not prepare their words beforehand—preparing only their thoughts—they save considerable time in sermon preparation. The two or three hours they save by not writing out a manuscript can be spent doing additional research for the sermon.

Presentation. In a sermon preached from a manuscript, I heard a preacher describe the witch of Endor as looking "like a wet gunnysack drooped over a fence post. One front tooth stood out like a lonely sentinel guarding the entrance to hell." Only wording prepared ahead of time can be that precise and descriptive.

Extemporaneous preaching from notes, however, is usually more relational and thus more preferred by most congregations. Henry Ward Beecher said that a written sermon reaches out a gloved hand to people; an unwritten sermon reaches out a glowing palm. A glove can be more perfect than the scarred and calloused hand, but it's not as warm, nor as sensitive.

Reading sermons limits the preacher's eye contact with the audience. Some manuscript preacher's heads go up and down like a chicken drinking. As we've suggested, preaching is truth through personality. Now, the eye definitely conveys personality. So anything that interferes with the preacher's eye contact keeps the personality from coming through and interferes with the preaching.

Manuscript preachers can offset some of the inherent weaknesses in their method by knowing the material so well that they do not have to read it word for word. They may read only parts of their sermon, preaching the rest of it extemporaneously. For example, illustrations and appeals don't lend themselves well to manuscript delivery and should probably be preached extemporaneously.

Easy? or effective? No single method fits everybody. And obviously both manuscript and extemporaneous preaching from notes have significant advantages and disadvantages. The problem is that preachers tend to choose the method that's wrong for them. It takes a vivacious and personable individual to read a sermon well. But it's the precise, scholarly person who is most likely to choose this method. Extemporaneous delivery, on the other hand, requires a good memory and careful organization that keeps the sermon moving and on a straight course. But it's the preacher of action, with less of a scholarly bent, who usually chooses this delivery.

Self-taught typists may learn to use just two fingers in a "hunt-and-peck" technique. Later in typing class, they feel totally uncomfortable using all the fingers as the teacher dictates and can hardly wait for her to turn her back so they can go back to what's more comfortable, even though it's less effective. You see, when we've done anything the wrong way often enough, it's the only way that feels right.

Too many of us preach the way we do because we have drifted into that technique and feel comfortable with it rather than because it's what communicates most effectively with our listeners. Choose the effective over the easy.

307-B. Prepare Everything Possible

The preaching event involves your ideas, your words, your notes, your Bible, your audience. Too much is going on at once and at a time you're suffering from too much stage fright to think straight. The least you can do to get ready for it is to prepare everything possible ahead of time.

As you prepare your notes or manuscript you might capitalize the most important parts so you can catch them at a glance. Or, underline significant words, perhaps with color, so you won't get lost in your notes. If you're going to turn to texts in your Bible, as you should for SDA audiences, cut up a little piece of card stock to drop in each passage ahead of time. Your Bible will open almost automatically to each text.

Do everything possible ahead of time so that when you preach you can forget the mechanics and remember the message.

308. Step 8: Prepare Yourself

Speaking of the very first Christian preachers, Ellen White wrote, "They were not authorized to preach a single discourse except under the influence of the Holy Spirit. They had strict orders to tarry in Jerusalem until they were endued with power from on high" *(Review and Herald,* June 3, 1902).

If you feel inadequate for the preaching task, that's good, providing you know what to do about it. "If any of you lacks wisdom, he should ask God, who gives generously to all without finding fault, and it will be given to him" (James 1:5).

No one appreciates speakers who talk farther than they walk. You don't have to be perfect to preach, but you must at least be perfectly committed to the truth you're preaching.

Here are some questions to pray over before you preach:

Is your life centered in Christ? Christianity is a relational religion. Too often we give people only something to believe. But God won't let them be satisfied until they have found someone to love, and that someone is Jesus Christ.

We mean to preach Christ-centered sermons and the only effective way to accomplish that is to be Christ-centered preachers. Say like Paul, "For I resolved to know nothing while I was with you except Jesus Christ and him crucified" (1 Cor.2:2).

Is your motive right? The ego is terribly at risk in the pulpit. If we do well, the devil will try to make us proud. If we do poorly he'll try to make us discouraged. Examine your motive in preaching. Is it to be helpful? or is it to be appreciated?

Do you love your listeners? The attitude of listeners toward a generally respected speaker is largely dependent upon what they believe the attitude of the speaker to be toward them—"Love me, and I'll love your message."

Can you love them even if your sermon doesn't seem to change them? We preach, expecting miracles. And rightly so. But the miracle of the slow-growing oak is just as great as the miracle of the overnight dandelion. Be patient with people who grow slowly. Oaks grow stronger than dandelions.

Preaching to a congregation is like throwing buckets of water over a room full of bottles. Some are wide-mouthed jars and some tiny-mouthed pop bottles. Don't be discouraged if most of the water ends up on the floor. Be encouraged that large amounts go into a few. Be hopeful that at least a little goes into each.

Is your objective clear? I notice that often when I hand my ticket to the agent at an airline ticket counter I'm asked, "And what is your final destination today?" It just doesn't make sense to set out on a journey without knowing where you're going.

Clear back in Step One, you determined the objective of your sermon. Where you wanted to go. What you wanted to have happen. Remind yourself again of that objective by laying your sermon before the Lord before you preach. Listen as the Holy Spirit whispers, "And what is your final destination today?" Never set out on a journey until you know where you're going.

Is your own heart moved by your message? There's an old legend that says

"The arrow dipped in your own blood speeds unerringly to its target." If you aren't moved by your message, chances are very slim that your congregation will be. We move others best with what's moved us most.

309. Step 9: Preach

We call it "delivering" the sermon. But what does that really mean? Feeling lazy, the paperboy dumps his bag of newspapers in the trash can rather than taking them to his subscribers. Have the papers been delivered? He has gotten them off his hands. But a thing is not really delivered until it has gotten into the hands of the person for whom it was intended.

Many sermons we preach never really get "delivered." We have gotten them out of our system, off our hands. But, perhaps because of the way we presented what we had to say, they didn't get into the minds of those for whom they were intended. They were preached, but not delivered.

Let's look very briefly at a few areas involved in sermon delivery:

309-A. Stage Fright

The most terrible time of all for beginning preachers may be when stage fright makes their knees go weak, their mouth go dry and their brain go numb. I remember how sympathetic my head elder was with me when I preached my first sermons as a ministerial intern. His heart went out to me because he sat behind me every Sabbath watching my knees shake.

Here are a few suggestions to help you handle stage fright:

Prepare diligently. If you have prepared conscientiously, know your message well and are enthusiastic about it, stage fright is diminished.

Breathe deeply. As you wait to begin, stage fright can cause hyperventilation and you take big, gulping breaths or breathe too fast and feel almost faint. Control this by purposely breathing slowly and deeply. This will both clear your mind and help you relax.

See Jesus by your side. As you step into the pulpit, imagine Jesus standing beside you. After all, it's His message you've prepared for the people. You're merely His mouthpiece. He never asks us to do anything that He won't help us accomplish.

Find some friendly faces. Some in your audience won't listen well. They'd be bored by the preaching of the Apostle Paul himself. Don't let them distract you or make you feel a failure. Find about three friendly faces of people who are listening encouragingly. The ideal is to find one on your right, one on your left, one in the center. By speaking to each of them in turn, you take in your whole audience.

Speak often. If you're serious about overcoming stage fright and becoming an effective speaker, try not to turn down invitations to speak. There's no solution to stage fright as effective as speaking often.

309-B. Use of Words

Carpenters build houses. They ought to have considerable knowledge about the principles of house construction. But they also need to know something about hammers and saws. Only through these tools can their knowledge produce houses.

Similarly, preachers ought to have considerable knowledge of Bible truth. But they also need to know something about words, for they are the tools by which that knowledge produces spiritual growth in their listeners.

In our use of words we must:

Be clear. The sermon is a telescope, not a kaleidoscope. The kaleidoscope draws attention to the bright bits of glass within itself. The telescope draws attention to that which is beyond itself. One you look at. The other you look through.

Clever wording is good but clear wording is essential. If you can be both clear and clever, great. But never sacrifice clarity for cleverness. Speak to be understood rather than to be admired.

Be accurate. Since we deal with such grand issues, preachers tend to overstate. People don't like that. In particular, watch out for *-est*. Not everything you talk about is the old*est*. bigg*est*, or great*est*. After we've exaggerated the earthly, people tend to assume we're still exaggerating when we speak of the heavenly.

Be included. Make a decision ahead of time about your use of pronouns. Use "we" often and "you" seldom. One of your advantages as a lay preacher is that, coming from the congregation, you speak for the congregation. As a fellow lay person, humbly include yourself as in need of the truths you preach.

Be yourself. Any airs or pretentiousness will detract. Either too ornate or too poor a use of words attracts attention to itself and away from your message.

Bathe your heart in the Holy Spirit so you have something helpful to say. Permeate your mind with good literature so you develop the vocabulary and use of words to say it well. Then step into the pulpit and speak it naturally.

309-C. Voice

So many of our churches now have microphones and sound systems that speaking to be heard is not as great a problem as in Ellen White's day. Nevertheless, her counsel is still very apropos, "With the voice we convince and persuade, with it we offer prayer and praise to God, and with it we tell others of the Redeemer's love. How important, then, that it be so trained as to be most effective for good.

"... There are many who read or speak in so low or so rapid a manner that they cannot be readily understood. Some have a thick, indistinct utterance; others speak in a high key, in sharp, shrill tones, that are painful to the hearers" (*Christ's Object Lessons*, p. 335).

One of the most practical points to remember in the use of voice is variety.

Any variation in rate, pitch or volume provides an attention step and helps your listeners listen.

309-D. Appearance

I put a small alarm-radio into my suitcase when I travel. Sitting alone in a lonesome corner of the world, I sometimes try tuning in some local music or news. Often, however, I'm at a church institution far away from cities and radio transmitters, and what I get is mostly static. Usually, I'll fidget and tune for a while trying to get rid of the noise, but if it's too persistent, eventually I'll simply turn the radio off.

In church, any of several forms of "static" often prevent people from hearing the good news about Jesus. This static might be unfriendly worshipers, a poor sound system, a crying baby, a stuffy room, or one that is too hot or cold. But the static I want to focus on here is that created by the preacher's physical appearance, dress and gestures. These externals always cause some static— they always interfere to some degree with what the preacher is saying. Sometimes the static becomes so loud the congregation hardly hears the sermon. And when there's too much static, people simply turn the preacher off.

Research indicates that when you preach, your listeners are more influenced by what they see than by what you say. Dr. Albert Mehrabian's research led him to insist that 7 percent of what speakers communicate comes from their words, 38 percent from their manner of speech, and 55 percent from the expressions on their faces and from their bodily movements. You may not like it, but your body language can speak so loudly your people hardly hear your sermons.

Now, if what people see in you reinforces what you say, all is well. The dilemma comes when your external communication interferes with what you are saying. You can hardly teach neatness and self-discipline while dressed like an unmade bed. You negate much of what you preach about self-control if you are grossly overweight. You can't portray the joy of following Christ if you preach with a frown on your face.

You might argue, "But appearance doesn't matter much to me." Does preaching matter to you? If it does, then appearance must matter, because what your people are seeing may speak so loudly they cannot hear what you are saying.

Keep your eye on your target. The eye is the window of the soul. When you look at your audience you share yourself with them. You create a sense of close contact, of friendship and intimacy. Every time you drop your eyes to read, to your audience it feels a little like the sun going behind a cloud.

Dress invisibly. Three helpful criteria for pulpit dress are neatness, good taste and simplicity. Nobody will ever criticize you for having your shoes shined and your clothes pressed. But if you don't, the precise and fastidious in your congregation may be so aggravated that they can hardly hear what you say. Now, you can complain about their overemphasis on externals, but you'll likely solve the problem a lot faster by shining your shoes and pressing your clothes.

The rule is that preachers should dress so nobody notices. If your appearance is cheap and shoddy, people notice. If your appearance is either too gaudy or too elegant, people notice. If you dress like 20 years ago or like 20 years in the future, people notice. Dress invisibly—in a way that your appearance does not distract from your message.

Gesture naturally. A good rule for use of gestures is *"See it, feel it and forget it."* See pictures in your mind as you prepare your sermon and you'll naturally use gestures to describe what you see.

Improved gestures most easily result, not from practicing more, but from feeling more. Feelings naturally find their expression in the sparkling eye, the contracted brow, compressed lips, or rigid muscles as the whole body speaks. Generally, the more you rely on notes the more difficult it is to feel your sermon and thus to use gestures.

A gesture must be the spontaneous product of present feeling or it will seem unnatural to you and ridiculous to your congregation. Form the habit of using meaningful gestures in daily conversation, then forget your gestures in the pulpit and just do what seems natural.

Smile. The sour-faced preacher leaves young people thinking, "I've got to fight off Christianity, or it might make me like that!" Be deadly in earnest, but don't look as if someone just died. Your face is an advertisement for what you are preaching. If there's a shine on your face, your people will try like everything to believe whatever is in your sermon, because they assume that following what you're saying will make them like you.

Beware of mannerisms. Mannerisms are not the exclusive property of the preacher. Watch the baseball pitcher as he prepares to pitch, the batter as he gets ready to hit, the basketball player at the free-throw line, or the tennis player about to serve. Almost invariably each will go through precisely the same routine of meaningless mannerisms just before putting the ball in play. These mannerisms are so deeply ingrained that the player is unaware of them, yet would feel completely unnatural without them.

Chances are, you'll unconsciously make many meaningless movements in the pulpit. You may move your Bible or notes, adjust your clothing, put your hands in and out of your pockets, or fidget with your glasses. These mannerisms probably feel as natural to you as the athletes' are to them. The problem is, your mannerisms may be so distracting that people have a hard time concentrating on your message.

One minister's wife always lined up the family to check the appearance of her husband and kids just before church. Her ritual included unfolding and checking her husband's handkerchief. She knew that one of his pulpit mannerisms was to thread his handkerchief back and forth between his fingers as he preached, and she was mortified at the thought of his doing it some day with a "holey" handkerchief.

My good wife used to get after me for putting a hand in my pants pocket and rattling the coins kept there. It seems silly to say, but I never knew I did it. However, I have finally learned to keep my hands out of my pockets when I preach. Your spouse may not be trained in Bible study or preaching, but he or she will pick up on distracting mannerisms in a hurry. The only problem is whether he/she dares tell you—and whether you care enough to change.

309-E. Transitions

One of the most awkward moments in preaching can come when we make transition from one part or segment of the sermon to the next. As you prepare, settle on a plan for making transitions that fits this particular sermon most naturally. Options include:

1. *Numerical*—"First, . . ." "Second, . . ." Third, . . ."

2. *Rhetorical*—"Why does God love us?" "Does God love Christians more than non-Christians?"

3. *Expository*—Read the next portion of your passage.

4. *Geographical*—"Upper Room," "Gethsemane," "Caiaphas' Courtyard."

5. *Recapitulate and announce.* That is, repeat the lesson of the present segment, show how it teaches the theme, then announce the lesson of your next segment. For example, the sermon outlined in Section 511 could make the transition from I-B to II something like this: "And so we can rest assured that the Good Shepherd understands and removes the need for fear. (The lesson of the present segment.) You see, we can depend on the Good Shepherd. (The theme.) Now notice that His way pays. (The lesson of your next segment.)"

This method is in many ways the most ideal. We must never assume that, having said something, everybody heard it or retains it. When reading, you can always go back and reread to pick up the thought. In oral communication, your listeners can't do that. Now, you don't want to repeat everything and bore your people. But if your theme and segment lessons have significant depth, recapitulation will make them clearer and improve your listeners' chances of taking them home.

309-F. Speaking Naturally

As the story goes, someone in awe of the centipede's ability to move all those legs to get around, asked him how he did it. This got the centipede to thinking so much about how and when each leg should move, that he became so confused he couldn't walk at all.

In the pulpit, if you concentrate on your use of words, voice, eye contact and gestures and all the nuances of sermon delivery you'll hardly be able to concentrate on your message at all. The time to think about all these is before you preach, not as you preach.

Long years of experience have led you to develop a way of speaking that has proven acceptable in everyday conversation. As a beginner in the pulpit, use that conversational style and you'll feel most comfortable and be most effective.

310. Step 10: Critique

Your sermon's been preached. Hopefully, the Lord has used you. But what has been most and least effective? How could you do it better next time? Again, ego gets in the way. People say nice things about the sermon and that's what we want to hear. Unfortunately, that's not always the best way to grow. Appreciate offhand remarks such as those made at the door as people leave church, but don't take them too seriously. They represent encouragement, not evaluation; custom, not critique.

Critique is essential, for there is little growth without struggle. To grow, preaching must be followed by evaluation, followed by preaching again, followed by evaluation again, etc. Here are some ways to get an accurate, honest evaluation:

310-A. Partner Evaluation

Spouse. Hopefully, your spouse is both an accurate and honest critic. Even spouses with no training in preaching can critique pulpit mannerisms, and probably will if encouraged. They can sit on the outside aisle during the sermon where they can see the audience as you preach, making note of what does and doesn't seem effective.

Group. Ask a friend to form a heterogeneous group to sit around a table after church with a tape recorder. You should not be present. The chairperson goes around the table asking each of perhaps five questions:

1. What did the sermon say?
2. What difference will it make in your everyday life?
3. What was the strongest thing about the sermon?
4. What was the weakest thing about the sermon?
5. What idea about preaching would you most like to share?

If the group does poorly on #1, your theme didn't get across. If they hesitate on #2, perhaps the sermon wasn't practical enough. You'll likely find they'll be reluctant to say anything negative about your sermon, but will become quite vocal on #5. They might teach you quite a bit about what they want most in preaching.

Later, you sit down, possibly with your spouse or another friend, and listen to the recording.

Congregation. A congregation is reluctant to critique a sermon. Some will feel it's almost sacrilegious. But there is an accurate way to learn what your listeners learned and, at the same time, contribute to their worship experience.

At the close of the sermon ask listeners to quietly question what they believe the Holy Spirit means to teach them this morning. Then have them write, "The sermon thought that will be most helpful to me this week is: . . ." Your reading these later will tell you a lot about your preaching.

310-B. Personal Evaluation

By all means evaluate your own sermon, but don't try either personal evaluation or listening to the evaluation of others until the sermon has had a little time to "cool." It's like criticizing a newborn baby to its mother while she's suffering from postpartum blues.

After a few hours or days, sit down and learn what you can from such evaluations as those suggested above. Or simply sit with a tape recording of the sermon and evaluate it alone, with your spouse, or with some other insightful friend.

I always grade each sermon. Recently, I've found it more effective to evaluate each segment separately and write an A, B, or C grade in the margin. If I want to preach the sermon again, I'll make sure to rework those segments with the lowest grade.

310-C. Preserving Everything

Write down everything you've learned. Write on the sermon what you've decided would improve it. Also, the sources you used, the place and date preached and the length. You may want to give the sermon a grade.

Gather your 3x5's and store them away with your sermon. Now, everything is preserved and available in case you ever want to rework the sermon and preach it again.

Chapter 4

A Working Summary

We've now covered so much so quickly you may be feeling a little overwhelmed. The 10 simple steps in sermon preparation that I promised may not seem so simple. The purpose of this chapter is to review those 10 through a workshop approach. That is, instead of discussing how it's done, we're going to do it.

This chapter will be of limited value unless you get out your Bible and prepare along with me a sermon you actually intend to preach. If you take the assignment seriously, by the end of the chapter you will have worked your way through all 10 of our steps and prepared a sermon. Then I'll show you the sermon I prepared and you can compare it with yours. Remember, you cannot learn preaching by reading—only by doing.

We're going to take a rather rigid approach to the 10 steps, to help you learn the necessity and advantage of each. Later, as sermon preparation becomes for you more natural and seems more possible, you'll no doubt adapt the 10 steps to your own gifts and personality.

401. Step 1: Choose Your Bible Passage or Topic

First, I must decide on my specific objective in preaching this sermon. What I want to do is show the relationship between Christ forgiving us and our forgiving others. I want to lead my listeners to accept Christ's forgiveness, then forgive others as He has forgiven them.

This will be an expository sermon. It's probably the easiest sermon type to keep biblical and to work through as an example of sermon preparation.

I've been reading the parables of Jesus and am moved by both their depth and practicality. I'm especially intrigued by the parable of The Unmerciful Servant and choose Matthew 18:21-35 as our passage.

402. Step 2: Study Your Passage to Find
Segment Lessons and Proofs

We want to come up with some good sermon segments (lesson, proof, illustration/application). (See Section 207-A, B.) But for now we'll concentrate on just lesson and proof as we work our way through the passage. For some, we may find illustrations right away. For others, illustrations will come in Step Three.

First, we read the passage rapidly several times answering the questions suggested in Section 302-A. I suggest you do this for yourself at this juncture and write down your answers to the three questions before you look at my answers.

My answers: 1—It seems to me the passage is about treating others as we've been treated. 2—I think Christ is teaching that Christians should treat the guilt of others as He treats ours. 3—The difference the passage makes is that it gives solutions for the very practical problems of guilt and forgiveness. Your answers are probably a bit different and very possibly better.

One of the things we learn from a rapid reading is that the parable is in four basic parts: the servant is guilty, he is forgiven, he refuses to forgive, the debt or guilt is reinstated. Right away we have a possible outline. Put it down on your 8 1/2- x 11-inch sheet. (See Section 302-B.)

Now let's read the passage slowly, carefully, meditatively. Look for key words, words that seem especially significant, or that are used most often. Notice the parable begins (vs. 21) and ends (vs. 35) with the word "forgive." That word seems to introduce and sum up the parable. "Pay" or "pay back" is used extensively. Do you find other key words you think are significant?

The immediate context is simple to find. Peter is asking how often we must forgive (vs. 21).

Lesson 1: Jesus answers that *forgiveness must be heartfelt, not mechanical* (vs. 35). We have our first lesson and proof. Let's put it down on our first 3x5. (See 302-B.) Note some other lessons and proofs as we study through our passage:

Lesson 2: *We stand guilty before God* (vs. 23, 24). The debt was real. The servant owed it. He was guilty. Put it on a 3x5.

Lesson 3: *We must give an account.* Verse 23 says the king "wanted to settle accounts." Another 3x5.

Lesson 4: *There's no human solution to our guilt.* Verse 25, "he was unable to pay." Another 3x5.

Lesson 5: *Christ's compassion brings forgiveness.* The "master took pity on him, canceled the debt and let him go" (vs. 27, 33). Another 3x5.

Lesson 6: *Others abuse us less than we abuse God.* Verses 24 and 28 compare 10,000 talents with 100 denarii. Later we'll turn to a Bible commentary to translate those amounts into present currency. Yes, life abuses us, and it hurts.

But nobody will ever be as indebted to us as we are to God. Another 3x5.

Lesson 7: *God expects us to model our compassion and forgiveness after His* (vs. 33). Servant B makes the same plea in verse 29 as servant A made in verse 26. But the master's treatment of A in verse 26 is totally different from A's treatment of B in verse 30. Another 3x5.

Lesson 8: *The unforgiving are unforgiven* (verse 34).

These are examples of lessons and proofs from our passage. How many more can you find? Can you find hope in the passage? Can you find Christ? Write each thought on a separate 3x5.

Turning to a topical Bible, I look up "guilt" and "forgiveness." One helpful verse I find is Psalm 40:12, where David, a man after God's own heart, is overwhelmed by guilt. Until we are overwhelmed by our guilt, we'll never be overwhelmed by God's grace. Another 3X5.

Now we look through some Bible commentaries, beginning with Ellen White's chapter on this parable in *Christ's Object Lessons*, "The Measure of Forgiveness." We find Jesus enlarged on lesson 8 above in Matthew 6:12 and 7:2. What other lessons or enlargement of lessons can you find in her chapter?

The *SDA Commentary* tells us A owed about $6,000,000 and B about $11.30. Another commentary points out: *God calls us wicked, not for how we've treated Him, but our fellowman* (verse 32). Another 3x5.

We've now established what the Bible is teaching about guilt and forgiveness and are free to enlarge on these principles by looking at some secular sources where we learn some differences between good guilt and bad guilt. Also, some ideas about the seriousness of guilt and how we can forgive. Remember to write every idea on a separate 3x5. Meanwhile, if the idea suggests a possible theme or outline, note it on your 8 1/2- x 11-inch sheet.

403. Step 3: Add Illustrations/Applications to Complete Your Segments

Most of our material is gathered now, except for illustrations/applications. Leaving the sermon for a while I let it simmer in the back of my mind for a few days. Later, I remember having had a car accident because I was looking behind instead of ahead. We can't live in the past and be happy in the present. I always carry 3x5 paper. Write it down before it gets away.

I remember visiting a leprosarium where people hurt themselves because they were unable to experience pain. Guilt is like pain. Though it hurts, it helps by warning us something's wrong. Another 3x5.

In a book of illustrations I find the illustration, "God not only cast my sins into the depths of the sea, He posted a notice, 'Fishing Prohibited'." It's unChristian to go through life feeling guilty.

Sitting at the dinner table I get to thinking about an overflowing cup and come up with the idea that whatever fills the cup overflows the cup. So, when someone's cup tilts and spills a drop of poison that hurts us, we should remember it's because they're full of the same hurting poison.

What illustrations/practical applications can you come up with that will help teach your lessons and apply them to your listeners' everyday lives? Again, write each on a 3x5.

Now it's time to fill out our segments. Lay your lesson and proof 3x5's on your table or desk and place each illustration/application 3x5 under the lesson it fits.

404. Step 4: Choose Theme and Outline

By now your 8 ½- x 11-inch sheet should be scribbled full of potential themes and outlines. It's time to choose your theme, the one sentence that gives the gist of your entire sermon. (See Section 302-C.) You may want to combine some of your potential themes to come up with one that really says what you want to say. The theme I'm choosing is, *Christ expects us to deal with others' guilt as He deals with ours*.

Next, I choose my outline from the same 8 ½- x 11-inch sheet. I settle on a chronological outline. That is, one that simply starts at the beginning of the passage and carries us through it in the same order as the passage is written:

    I. The Christian begins with guilt
   II. The Christian moves from guilty to forgiven
  III. The Christian moves from forgiven to forgiving

Note that each division relates to the theme and builds on the division before it. Can you come up with a theme and outline that you particularly want to preach?

405. Step 5: Organize Your Sermon

Next, we look through our 3x5's to find ideas that will fit our introduction and conclusion.

In the introduction we want to gain attention to our topic and theme, make people want to listen. The one I choose is probably a little shorter than most. It begins by calling attention to Jesus' story, then gives a pre-summary by suggesting the lessons of the three main divisions, and climaxes with the theme.

In the conclusion we want to summarize, make a call to action and prepare our final words so we have a plan for getting sat down. I'm going to summarize by highlighting the three divisions, then use a practical illustration about forgiving which will lead to the call to action. The final words will be a slight rewording of the theme, "The true test of Christian character is how close we come to treating others' guilt as Christ has treated ours."

After you've given some thought to your introduction and conclusion, put each part of your outline on a separate 3x5 and lay these across the top of your desk or table. In my case, I'll write this in red to differentiate the outline from the material that goes under it. From left to right, I'll put five 3x5's: Introduction, Christian begins with guilt, Christian moves from guilty to forgiven, Christian moves from forgiven to forgiving, Conclusion.

Under Introduction and Conclusion I'll place any 3x5's that fit. Then each segment will go under the proper division heading.

Using the outline you've chosen, you should now lay out your own outline and material as suggested above.

406. Step 6: Change and Delete

Does your material fit your tentative outline and theme? Now is the time to change the theme and revise the outline to fit your segments. No matter how good a theme, it must be revised to fit your material. You can't preach on a theme about which you have nothing to say. If you have too many segments for one part of your outline and too few for another part, either change the outline or eliminate some segments.

This is the time to consider your sermon length. In my case, I'll delete the poorest material until I come up with about 25 3x5's. This will give me a 25-30 minute sermon.

Be ruthless. Throw out the B ideas. Take out the A ideas that don't fit this sermon and save them for another time. Your sermon is likely to become an A or a B sermon depending on how carefully you weigh and delete at this juncture.

407. Step 7: Write Out Your Notes or Manuscript

Choose your sermon title. I'm torn between "Good Guilt" and "Forgiven-Forgiving." As I prepare the notes I'll take into the pulpit, I'll underline, capitalize, bold or mark with color the main ideas so I can almost preach the sermon just from these. This also keeps me from getting lost in my notes while preaching. I'll mark my Bible as suggested in Section 307-B. I know I'm not bright enough to say anything substantial while hunting for my next text.

408. Step 8: Prepare Yourself

My sermon is prepared. But am I? It's time to pray that my life will be centered in Christ so I can preach a Christ-centered sermon. Are my motives right? After all the work I've done on this sermon, is my objective still clear? Have I applied my message to myself so my own heart is moved?

409. Step 9: Preach

Under Section 309 we talked about a whole host of important things involved with successful sermon delivery: stage fright, use of words, voice, appearance. But the time to concern yourself with these is before and not during your sermon. Just be yourself and concentrate on your message.

You do need to make some plans about transitions from one part of your sermon to another. Section 309-E gives suggestions. If you don't come up with something you're sure will work better, close each segment by repeating the lesson, then repeat the theme if it fits, then announce the lesson of your next segment. (See Section 309-E.) If your lessons have depth, telling your listeners what you're going to tell them, then telling them, then telling them what you told them makes preaching more understandable and effective.

410. Step 10. Critique

Whether or not you choose to use any of the other critique methods suggested in Section 310, I would encourage you to at least tape record your sermon and listen to it a few days later either alone or with an insightful friend.

As suggested in Section 310-C, write on your sermon anything that would improve it if you were to use it again. File your 3x5's away with the sermon so that all your previous research is available in case you decide to rework it later. The best sermons of the best preachers are those they've preached over.

Chapter 5

Sample Sermons and Sermon Outlines

Sections 501-530 below are from sermons I have preached and are included as examples of the theory in this book. Many have been referred to already. Sections 501-510 are sermons, slightly abbreviated. Sections 511-530 are sermon outlines that might serve as sermon seeds from which you could grow your own sermons.

Just before each title there is a little explanation regarding the sermon or outline. This includes the sermon type (see Section 206) and, where appropriate, the passage, topic and homiletics lessons taught.

Some Scripture verses used are followed by an "a" which means the first part of the verse, or a "b" meaning the middle, or a "c" meaning the last part. There is nothing sacred about chapter or verse structures in Scripture. Sometimes the same verse teaches several lessons, in which case the listener should not be distracted by your reading those parts of the verse that introduce a lesson you're not presently teaching.

Some texts are in parenthesis. This indicates that these should probably be studied in preparing the sermon, but not read in the pulpit. There are examples of this in Section 501.

The sermons have been somewhat abbreviated to save space. Lessons and themes are seldom repeated at the end of segments, but should often be added when the sermon is delivered.

If you find reason to preach from these sermons or outlines, Ellen White has these words of wisdom, "Do not trust to the wisdom of any man, or to the investigations of any man. Go to the Scriptures for yourselves, search the inspired word with humble hearts, lay aside your preconceived opinions; for you will obtain no benefit unless you come as children to the word of God. You should say, 'If God has anything for me, I want it. If God has given evidence from his word to this or that brother that a certain thing is truth, he will give it to me. I can find that evidence if I search the Scriptures with constant prayer, and I can know that I do know what is truth.' You need not preach the truth as a product of another man's mind, you must make it your own" (*Review and Herald*, March 15, 1890).

501. Forgiven-Forgiving

[An expository sermon based on Jesus' Parable of the Unmerciful Servant in Matthew 18:21-35. Topic: forgiveness. Emphasizes Christian's moving from guilty to forgiven to forgiving.]

Introduction

Let's look at one of the most fascinating, least understood stories Jesus ever told. We'll learn that true Christianity progresses from guilty, to forgiven, to forgiving.

Theme: *Christ expects us to deal with others' guilt as He deals with ours.*

I. **Christian begins with guilt.**
   A. **We are guilty**—Matt. 18:23, 24—debt was real. He was guilty. Psalmist said, ". . . my sins . . . are more than the hairs of my head" (Ps. 40:12). How many hairs, David? Too many to count. How much guilt? Too much to measure. Man after God's own heart was one who had been overwhelmed by guilt. Great danger in being respectable, hard working, commandment-keeping Christian, we're more likely to feel proud than guilty. *Until overwhelmed by our guilt, never overwhelmed by His grace.* Guilt has gotten a bad reputation, but there's both good and bad.
   B. **Shun bad guilt.**
      Driving my car while watching rear view mirror, I bumped into the car that stopped in front of me. Learned it's dangerous to be continually looking back. We *can't live in past and be happy in present.* Bad guilt: perpetually looking back, guilt that makes you feel a failure, guilt for which you know no solution.
   C. **Embrace good guilt.**
      At Malamulo leprosarium, Malawi, I saw patients terribly scarred, but it wasn't directly from leprosy. It was because leprosy had numbed their limbs so they had bruised or burned themselves without knowing it. *Guilt, like pain, though it hurts, helps by warning something's wrong.* Pop psychology says guilt is to be avoided. But examining behavior in our homes, on our streets, at our public offices, we learn society is suffering, not too much sense guilt, but too little. When you do bad thing, feel guilty. Good for you, and rest of us that have to live with you. But to have done a

bad thing doesn't make you bad person. Good guilt is when we *regret our behavior, respect ourselves.*

II. Christian moves from guilty to forgiven.
Christianity must begin with guilt or there's no forgiveness, but it would be a sick religion if it left us there.

A. No adequate human solution to guilt—vs. 25—"not able to pay." Guilt continued breaks us mentally, physically, spiritually. Christianity offers release.

B. Christ's compassion brings forgiveness—vs. 26, 27. Former derelict, "God not only cast my sins into depths sea, He posted notice "Fishing Prohibited." It's unChristian to go on feeling guilty for sins Christ has removed. Fishing prohibited!

We say, "That's nice. I was guilty, but now forgiven. I've learned the parable's lesson." But only part way through the story. We've moved from *guilty* to *forgiven*, but our third word is *forgiving*. Too many go no further. They're only two-thirds Christian.

III. Christian moves from forgiven to forgiving.
A. Though others abuse us, it's less than we abuse God—vs. 28-30 10,000 talents = 6 million dollars; 100 denarii = $11.30. We all muddle our way through life where people are forever hurting one another. Friend betrays us, parent abuses, spouse rejects. Their indebtedness, abuse serious; but we indebted God for every heartbeat, every breath take. When tempted to self pity, remember we owe God 6 million, compared to $11.30 others owe us.

B. Christ expects us to deal with others' guilt as He deals with ours vs. 31-33—"mercy on your fellow servant just as I had on you?" "wicked" not because how treated God, but fellowman. Some Christians who claim to love God, can't stand people *not forgiving, not forgiven*—vs. 34—debt was reinstated. Jesus repeated in Lord's Prayer (Matt. 6:12)—"Forgive us our debts as we forgive our debtors." Small boy didn't quite understand Lord's Prayer, but he still made sense when he prayed "forgive us our debts as we forgive those who are dead against us."

C. Forgiveness must be heartfelt, not mechanical
vs. 21—"seven times"—Peter's forgiveness mechanical
vs. 35—"from your heart"—Jesus' forgiveness heartfelt
How can I be heartfelt forgiver? Three suggestions:
1. *Face your anger, resentment*—Christians feel shouldn't have, so deny. Think if swallow it, ready translation—really ready crazy house. Hiding resentment rather than facing, unChristian.
2. *Realize consequences of refusing to forgive. Hatred hurts the hater more than the hated.* Your memory becomes videotape, sending through your mind unending reruns of pain. Only forgiveness

erases tape. Set prisoner free. The prisoner is yourself.
3. *Understand the offender*. What was the offender's intent? People
hurt people, but seldom purposely. Jesus used: "Father forgive
. . . *know not what they do*" (Luke 23:34). Life like overflowing
cup. Whatever fills cup, overflows the cup. Can't fill cup with
poison and overflow orange juice. Next time someone's cup spills
a drop poison on you, don't just complain, "Ouch, you hurt me!"
Rather, say to yourself, "Wow, if one drop hurts so much, how
much that person must hurt, being full of it."

Conclusion

Christ expects us deal with others' guilt as He deals with ours. Christianity
means moving. Not a stagnant, onetime experience. Begins *guilt*, little guilt
little appreciation forgiveness. Must never end there. Move to be *forgiven*.
"Fishing prohibited." Show your appreciation by **forgiving,** treating others
guilt as Christ treated yours.

Tom a husky 22-year-old husband, father. Surly, brooding, short-tempered
with two children, trouble holding job. Went to psychotherapist for 8 months.
Learned problem stemmed from alcoholic father who had belittled him. But
therapist couldn't get him any farther. Frustrated, Tom went to his pastor,
who suggested, "Why don't you try forgiving your father?" Prayed together
and Tom sensed burden lifted, remarkable newness. Went to father, "Last night
I asked God help me forgive you. Think worked." Cried together, embraced,
healing began.

Give Christ your *guilt*, accept His *forgiveness*, begin to *forgive*. *True test
of Christian character is how close we come to treating others guilt as Christ
has treated ours.*

502. Invincible

[An expository sermon based on a psalm, Psalm 46. Topic: dependence on
God. Example of outlining an entire psalm, good theme and main divisions.]

Introduction

SDA church is facing significant problems:
Aging problem—movement over 150 years old. Most reformation
movements begin to fade after third and fourth generation.
Nationalism problem—hard be world church when every country
feels it must have its own way; where some feel it's unchristian to
ordain women and others feel it's unchristian not to.
Change problem—conservative can't live with change, progressive can't
live without change.

But only one *critical* problem. All others peripheral: will we let God run His church? So critical because:

Theme: *Nothing can destroy what's in God's hands.*

Look at song from old church hymnal, Psalm (song) 46.
Introduction says the song was presented to music director, for choir, with soprano solo. Three stanzas, each ending with Selah.
First stanza:

I. **Christian calm amidst calamity when God present**—Ps. 46:1-3.
   A. **Not promise to prevent trouble, but to be present when trouble comes** vs. 1 "ever-present help in trouble." Never teach Christian calm because no trouble when God present. Unfair hold it against God for failing to keep promises He never made. His promise is not prevention, but presence.
   B. **Every physical (human) refuge eventually fails—**
      vs. 2, 3 "mountains."—Whenever a significant Bible word is mentioned more than once in a short passage we expect it to be important. Notice that mountains are mentioned twice. Mountains are nature's fortresses, immovable, unshakable. The Psalmist is asking, "What will you do when the unshakable shakes?"
      Every physical, every human refuge eventually fails. I know a father who loved to throw his baby into air. Every time went up, baby laughed. Every time came down, father caught, except once. Head hit concrete and never laughed again. Every human refuge eventually fails. Some refuge failed, some hurt pressing every heart here: death of loved one, loveless marriage, child left Lord, health that's failing, work that isn't working. But "God is our refuge" (vs 1a) No wonder this psalm led Martin Luther to write, "A mighty fortress is our God, A bulwark never failing." Every physical (human) refuge eventually fails—but Jesus never fails.
   Second stanza:

II. **The Church is invincible when God is present**—vs. 4-7.
   A. **God is in His church**—vs. 4a "There is a river." Ancient cities invincible because built on river: Babylon on Euphrates, Nineveh on Tigris. But Jerusalem was not built on a river. She was to depend only on God. Modern Israel likewise.
   B. **God is in His church at every level**—vs. 4a "a river whose streams." River produces power, but streams produce life. Ideally, tributaries were taken off rivers of ancient cities so a little water came to every home's garden and that's where things grew. There's no baptistry at GC office, nor division, union or local conference. But there's likely one in your church. Church grows, not at the centers of power, but

in local congregation.

C. **Church's temptation, keep God nearby rather than within**—on periphery rather than at center. vs. 5a "in the midst of her" (KJV). Church wants God. What is city without water? But a river in the center of town can be a nuisance. Handier nearby where go when needed, but not be controlled by when inconvenient. When God is in control we lose control. It's against human nature to voluntarily give up control. Especially hard for leaders to be led. They're used to leading. Against our nature give up independence. You rescue baby bird just before cat pounces. The cat can't destroy what's in your hands. How does bird feel? "Turn me loose!" Depending on you is against its nature.

D. **Only God's presence makes the church invincible**—vs. 5b "she will not fall." City not invincible because of guards, gates, but river. Church not invincible because of people, pastors, plans, or prophetic promises—but God.

Third stanza:

III. **Practice God's presence in both good times and bad**—vs. 8-11.

A. **When things go *right* take time to look for God.** We become acquainted with God by observing the acts of God. vs. 8, 9—we view battlefield after the battle. God has broken every weapon used against us. Each should create that kind of "Book of Remembrance." We'll need it later.

B. **It takes time to ponder God's goodness**—vs. 10a "be still and know." If can't be still may never know. Get so busy, even in work of Lord, neglect Lord of work. Gas truck pulled off highway, out of gas. Had given gas all up and down the countryside until had none left for itself. We so busy giving family, work, church we become empty ourselves.

C. **When things go *wrong* remember that what He's done before He can do again**—vs. 11 "Lord Almighty is with us." It's not just that He's almighty, but that that kind of God is with **us**. Don't be frightened when you or church attacked. It's easier to head for fortress. The more God does for us the less we tend to appreciate Him. There never has been real revival in midst of prosperity. Let calamity come if it will drive us to the fortress.

Conclusion

Nothing can destroy what's in God's hands. Only way our church can be in God's hands is if we are. Dependable old bitch had been leader of sled-dog team in Alaska. Owner experimented by replacing with young, energetic leader. All went well until driver noticed his boot needed tying. Stopped sled but failed to set brake. When bent down to tie boot the new leader headed for home. Owner gave call for team to turn and circle back toward him, but headstrong leader refused. Into Eskimo village came most unusual sight— driverless sled, with something flopping back and forth. It was the old leader who had tried so hard to turn team she'd gotten tangled in harness and choked to death. Buried her in place of honor in dog cemetery—the one who gave her life trying to pull others back to her master. Won't you rededicate your life to calling your church, calling men and women, boys and girls back to the Master! For nothing can destroy what's in God's hands.

503. Designed for Heaven

[Expository sermon based on first and last 2 chapters of Bible. Topic: heaven. A youth sermon. Note the intimacy between theme and divisions and how the theme is used in making transitions from one division to the next.]

Introduction
Preacher asked boy, "Sonny, do you want to go to heaven?" "Huh, uh." "What, you don't want to go to heaven when you die?" "Oh, when you die. I thought you was makin' up a load to go now."

Just about everybody wants to go to heaven—but please, Lord not too soon. It sounds like a great place if you get sick, better and better as we get older and older, and an absolute must when we die. Youth want Jesus to come, but not until married and lived their lives. We seem to feel, "Please come, but not so soon you spoil my fun."

What would living in a sinless world be like? There are basically four chapters in the Bible depicting a sinless world: Genesis 1 and 2, before sin came; Revelation 21 and 22, after sin ends. All the rest of Scripture describes a tragic, sinful interlude. The devil has fooled us into thinking heaven a place where feel out place. Actually, heaven only place ever feel completely at home.

Theme: *Designed for heaven, we'll never function fully till we get there.*

I put on some snorkeling gear and enjoyed swimming with the fish. But every fish there could outswim me. Put the fish on land and it flops around totally graceless. We function well only in the environment for which we were designed. Designed to live in a sinless world, we can get by and function partially in sinful world, but we'll function fully only in the world for which we were designed. Five examples showing we were designed for a different world from the one in which we live:

I. **Designed for life, we hate death.**
   Why so many jokes about the perfectly respectable profession of

undertaker? Because we abhor death so that we're embarrassed by the person who chooses to live with it. As I stood by my mother's open grave, I knew I could never feel good again about living in a world where there's death.

A. **In Eden, only life**—Gen. 1:11. Provision only for life. Every time we eat a watermelon we should be reminded of God's intention. Seeds to the right and seeds to the left illustrate God's overwhelming provision for life.

B. **In heaven, death abolished**—Rev. 21:4. Our cat failed to come home one night. Next morning my wife headed for work before me and called home saying there was a black cat dead on the road that looked like our Panther. Dutifully, I checked out the dead cat but it was obviously not ours. (Panther came home when he was good and ready.) But nobody's cat deserves what happens to it if left on the road. I must admit I had to screw up my courage some to lift that mangled cat carcass and give it a decent burial in the ditch. Why? We're repulsed by death because we were made for life. Designed for heaven, we'll never function fully till we get there.

II. **Designed for love, we dread loneliness**—Gen. 2:18.
God allowed no loneliness in Eden. We don't have to be married to be happy. Unfortunately there are almost as many unhappy married people as unhappy singles. But you do have to feel loved. Creator gave everyone desire be with someone and everyone someone be with. Except Adam. Little girl was told that Eve was an afterthought. She replied, "No! God made Adam first. Then he stood back and said, 'If I tried again I think I could do better'. Then He made Eve."

Why the apparent separation between the creation of Adam and of Eve? Bible says God sent Adam out to play with the animals. Maybe Adam saw a Mr. and Mrs. Lion, goose, wolf, cardinal, until he felt he was missing something. Only then did God make Eve. Most men need time to learn they were created for love, that love beats freedom, independence, power. Girls must be patient like God was. Let them play with their Mustangs and Broncos and other horses under their hoods. Like Adam, they'll eventually learn that love is better.

If your heart is shrivelling from loneliness, give it to Jesus. For in His world, loneliness is not allowed. Designed for heaven, we'll never function fully till we get there.

III. **Designed to master nature, its unwillingness to be mastered frustrates us**—Gen. 1:26a, 28a "rule." Why do humans have the instinct to hunt and fish? Perhaps because we were designed to rule the fish and animal world and, since sin came, we can do so only with a gun or fishing rod. Why the planting and gardening instinct? In spring, thumbs turn green and we rush out to plant. But throughout the season we battle beetles and bugs, weeds and worms and by fall we become so frustrated we let the weeds take over. Designed to master nature, its unwillingness to be mastered frustrates us. Designed for heaven, we'll never function fully till we get there.

IV. **Designed to enjoy the sensual, sin makes sensuality an end in itself**— Gen. 2:9a "Pleasing to the eye"—the sense of sight. Why did Creator make flowers, sunsets? "Good for food"—the sense of taste. Why did God make taste buds? He could have designed us so we stepped up to a pump once a week, "Fill it up," and we'd get a week's worth of nutrients. No, God made eating a delightful experience. Our God is sensual, not just utilitarian.

I imagine Adam standing beside Eve beneath a tree in Eden. He *looks* up and the sky looks good, *hears* a bird singing and the bird sounds good, *smells* a flower and it smells good, bites into a piece of fruit and the fruit *tastes* good, reaches out to *touch* Eve and Eve feels good—and Adam feels at home. The devil didn't invent the senses. God's world is a sensual world.

Sensuality was meant to make the good life enjoyable. In our perverted, mixed up world, sin claims that sensuality makes the good life unnecessary. But when eat whatever we feel like, as much as we feel like, we're worshiping our senses rather than their Creator.

When we touch whatever we feel like, whenever we can get away with it, we feel hypocritical and empty at best and betrayed at worst. Sex with commitment is grand, a part of Creator's sensual plan. Without commitment it's destructive. Commitment is when we stand in front of our friends, family, God and say, "This one only, always." Only God's plan for sensuality works. Designed for heaven, we'll never function fully till we get there.

V. **Designed for variety, sameness bores us**—Rev. 22:2a—why 12 varieties of fruit on heaven's trees, when we have only one variety here? Perhaps it's to illustrate that there'll be 12 times as much variety there as here.

A. **Youth restless because designed for variety**. Our son had a Gordon Setter dog, designed to be a retriever, a water dog. Taffy loved her master's world, but she also loved world of water. She'd be playing with her master one moment, and the next be sloshing down the creek that ran behind the house. She wanted both worlds. Some young people are bored and restless in school where teachers are hard, so try the work world where they find bosses even harder. They dedicate all week to the world then give the Master an hour or two on Sabbath, wanting both worlds. The church doesn't satisfy them so they think they need the world. What they really need is the endless variety of God's world.

B. **Heaven isn't here**—In a sense, all of life is a quest for some kind of heaven. At different stages of life we look in different places. I remember when I thought heaven was having all the candy I could eat. One day I ate a whole bagful, all I could eat. But I got a sour stomach. Heaven wasn't there. Later, I thought heaven was a new car. Then I got a new car. In a few days it was dirty and started to rattle. The payments lasted longer than the car. Heaven wasn't there.

Some think heaven is getting married. But all marriage is temporary, ending at best in death, at worst in failure and divorce. Heaven isn't there. Others think that heaven is having a baby of your own. But babies grow up and leave you, sometimes with hardly a backward glance. Heaven isn't there. Others think heaven is a new house. But a house doesn't make a home. It demands all your extra time just to take care of it—and the payments and the taxes are terrible. Heaven isn't there. We're all sometimes tempted to think that heaven is retirement. But in retirement you begin to feel useless and watch as your body wears down and death creeps up. Heaven isn't here, it's only over there. Designed for heaven, we'll never function fully till we get there.

Conclusion

Summary: [repeat main divisions] designed for life, love, master nature, sensual, variety. Designed for heaven, we'll never function fully till we get there. A loving God wouldn't design you for heaven without making it possible for you to be there. Scripture's last invitation, Rev. 22:17 "whosoever will" (KJV). Your will the only thing keep from heaven. Not mistakes, Jesus can forgive. Not weaknesses, He'll help overcome.

Driving down highway I stopped when saw car pulled over on shoulder, stuck in mud. Wife driving, husband pushing. Several of us gathered around and found the car was almost down to its axle. We suggested that the husband drive. We got behind to push. Someone shouted, "Give it everything you've got." The motor roared, the wheels spun, the mud flew, we pushed. Quicker than it takes to tell the story they were out of the rut and on their way home.

Give Christ your will. Give Him your time, your talent. Give Him everything you've got. Before you know it we'll be out of this old rut of sin and on our way to the only home where we'll ever be completely at home. Designed for heaven, we'll never function fully till we get there.

504. Happiness and the Christian

[An expository sermon based on highlights from an entire Bible book—Ecclesiastes. Topic: happiness in Christ. Exemplifies use of positive and negative: first division what won't work, second division what will work. First

division's subdivisions have contrasting segments of "tried" and "result." Good
youth sermon.]

Introduction
   Humans come in widely assorted sizes, shapes and colors. Yet, different as
we are, be we young or old, rich or poor, Christian or atheist, all looking for
same thing—happiness. But happiness exceptionally elusive. Unhappiness
hard to get rid of. Frantic woman called constable in Owen Sound, Ontario.
Had skunk in her basement. How get rid of. Constable told her to make trail
bread crumbs from basement into woods, the skunk would follow and be gone.
She called again, more frantic. He asked if she'd made trail into woods. Yes.
What happened? Now had two skunks in basement. Harder we try get rid of
unhappiness, the more we sometimes have.

Theme: *We find happiness, not by seeking it, but by seeking Christ.*

   We can only be surprised by joy, even in Christianity. Seeking tends be
self-centered and we designed to be happy only when other-centered. "I looked
to Christ and dove of peace flew to my shoulder. I looked to the dove and it
flew away."

   I. **Happiness not found by seeking it.**
       Solomon dramatic example of someone learned lesson hard way. He
       was gifted, he was rich. Every avenue was available and tried every
       one. Ecclesiastes is story of his search and what he learned.
       A. **Entertainment won't bring happiness.**
           Tried: Eccl. 2:1a, pleasure. Drink, vs. 3a. Entertainment (his own floor
           show), vs 8b. Sex, vs 8c. He amassed 700 wives, 300 concubines. Just
           think of the time it would take him to kiss them all goodnight!
           Result: Eccl. 7:6—Entertainment like dry weeds in a fire, noisy and
           bright, but terribly temporary. Brought excitement, but not
           happiness. I watched fireworks display. The man-made stars were
           flashy and colorful, but temporary. When they went out I could still
           see God's stars pinned against black curtain of night. Less flash but
           more permanence, more staying power.
       B. **Knowledge won't bring happiness.**
           Tried: Eccl. 1:16, 17a. He was original renaissance man. Studied
           science, art, biology, poetry, psychology, philosophy.
           Result: Eccl. 2:14, 16c. He got to thinking about death. Any
           philosophy of life that doesn't answer problem of death is a dead
           end. Good for us to occasionally walk in cemetery and, like Solomon,
           confront the inevitability of death. We could study hour after hour,
           earn degree after degree, but grim reaper wipes all out instant bony
           finger touches heart with death. IQ of moron's corpse same as Solomon's.

C. **Work won't bring happiness.**
    Tried: Eccl. 2:4-6—now we're getting even closer to where a lot of us live. Many Christians tend to worship work ethic, feeling if work good, overwork must be better. Work from time climb out bed in morning to fall into bed at night. Presume "I'm too busy" excuses neglecting spouse, kids, private devotions. Overwork is sin Christians most likely proud of.
    Result: Eccl. 2:18,19. Realized can't take results of work with you. Heirs squander foolishly.

D. **Money won't bring happiness.**
    Tried: Eccl. 2:7, 8a. Imported Egyptian horses. I saw their mangers still in existence at Megiddo. (1 Kings 10) says silver as plentiful as stones on streets of Jerusalem.
    Result: Eccl. 5:10. Dr. R. F. Horton spent most of his life as pastor of wealthy London congregation: "The greatest lesson life has taught me is that people who set their mind and heart upon riches are equally disappointed, whether they get them or whether they do not get them."

E. **Solomon's summary: Nothing human brings total happiness—**
    Eccl. 2:11. Not entertainment, learning, work, money. One edition of *Prophets and Kings* has a picture of Solomon sitting on his throne with his head in his hand. The scepter has fallen to the floor, symbolizing that his wrong choices are about to result in the power of his throne being lost and his kingdom divided. A picture of life wasted seeking happiness in all the wrong places. Then, almost too late, life nearly ending, he finds the secret:

II. **Happiness is living for Christ.**
    Eccl. 2:26a—"God gives . . . happiness." "If you want joy, real joy, wonderful joy, let Jesus come into your heart." Rudyard Kipling gravely ill typhoid fever, surrounded by human love and medical genius, kept whispering something. Nurse bent down, "What do you want, Mr. Kipling?" "I want God." An emptiness in human soul, placed there by Creator, can be filled only by Himself.

A. **Whole only when Christ's**—Eccl. 12:13. When really thirsty, soda pop tickles nose, but only water really quenches. That thirst you have, quenched only by water of life.

B. **Whole only when *wholly* Christ's**—Eccl.10:1. Just a few dead flies getting into batch when perfume being made will make whole thing stink. Partial commitment stinks. Nine-12 Sabbath morning won't work.

Conclusion

We find happiness, not by seeking it, but by seeking Christ. Don't be like

Solomon, learning source of total happiness too late in life. In each of my hands I hold a key. Both are keys to my house. The key in my left hand will open garage door, but other doors I'm locked out. The master key in my right hand will open garage door, front door, back door, closet door, pantry door—every door. Christ is master key to happiness. Other keys may bring degrees of satisfaction, but only He can open every door, meet every need. Reach out right now and take hold of Christ, the master key. We find happiness, not by seeking it, but by seeking Christ.

505. Love? or Law?

[Expository sermon based on 10 commandments. Topic: love and law inseparable. Doctrinal sermon showing practicality of the law.]

Introduction

Employees at a Convair airplane plant in San Diego were proud of their safety record—176 days without an accident. But the record ended when a worker fell and broke his knee. Actually, what he did was fall over a safety first sign! Sometimes the very thing meant to help us, becomes our downfall. That can be true of the 10 commandment law. We don't want a loveless law, legalism. So we exchange it for a lawless love, an adaptation of "do your own thing" to Christian life. When I was young we had the law on the front wall of our churches, but crosses were not allowed. Today, we have the cross, but the law isn't allowed.

The beautiful Righteousness by Faith doctrine says we are saved by relationship, not behavior. It's true. It's important. But the sermon too often stops halfway through. We are saved by a relationship that changes behavior, a love for Christ that helps us want to follow and obey Christ. We separate love and law only when fail understand either, for they are inseparable. Actually,

Theme: *God's law applies love to life.*

Why 10 commandments? What is purpose of the law?
I. **Two reasons God gave us 10 commandments:**
   A. **Too show us what *God* is.** 10 commandments look at God from 10 different angles. All of you can see this pulpit. Yet none of us can see all of it. To see the whole pulpit we would need to view it from front side, back, top, bottom. Only then would we get a complete view. 10 commandments are 10 sides or facets of God. A transcript of His character. If we neglect them it limits our knowledge of what He's like and we create a God of our own imagination, an extension of

our own personality and preferences.

B. **To show us what** *love* **is.** 10 commandments define love. Christ summarizes the law in Mark 12:30, 31a. We like these two commandments of the New Testament better than the 10 of the Old Testament. They seem more gentle, liberal, open-ended. We all believe in love so long as **we** can decide what it is. Our problem with the 10 commandments is that they make love so specific and practical it interferes with our selfish instincts.

   True love leads to changed behavior. Love is genuine only in action. 10 commandments show love isn't just pretense, emotion, sentimentalism, sex, way to sell soup or soap. Ten commandments are love in action. God's definition of what real love really is.

   Let's look at each of the 10 and notice:

II. **Every commandment applies love to life.**
Commandment One: Ex. 20:3 "You shall have no other gods before Me" shows:

A. **Love means putting God first.** Life really works only when God is at its center. God does not want to be our only love, but our first love. He does not ask us to love Him *instead* of our fellowman. A selfish child climbs up on father's lap and looks down, taunting the less favored siblings on the floor. Religious fanatics feel they are so close to God they look down with a negative, critical attitude at those they feel are less favored. But there's no way we can get so close to God it separates us from people. God wants to be the hub of our wheel, with all other relationships spokes of the wheel. Fastening spokes to the hub gives them strength. Putting God first strengthens relationship spouse, child, neighbor, boss, church member.

Commandment Two: vs. 4 "You shall not make for yourself an idol in the form of any*thing*" shows:

B. **Love means worshipping a person—not things.** Idol is a thing, and God wants us to put persons before things. He doesn't want us to waste our worship on a god that can't love us back

Commandment Three: vs. 7 "You shall not misuse the name of the Lord your God" shows:

C. **Love means defending God's good name.** He wants His name to stand for hope, acceptance, love—not hate, filth, anger. It hurts Him to hear "God damn you", yet He hears it 1,000 times to one "God loves you." Meanwhile, He's 1,000 times more willing to love us than damn us.

Commandment Four: vs. 10 "the 7th day is a Sabbath *to the Lord your God*. On it you shall not do any work" shows:

D. **Love means Sabbath togetherness with God**. We don't stop work in order to do nothing, but in order to start worshipping, spending the day with God. What are proper things to do on Sabbath?

Anything that focuses on God. We can break the Sabbath even in church if focus on building, preacher, or hypocrite in pew.

Commandment Five: vs. 12 "Honor your father and your mother" shows:

E. **Love means honoring family ties.** "Honor . . . your mother." What a revolutionary idea! In the world around Sinai, women were the playthings of the rich or the burden bearers of the poor. God said that, among His people, they were to be honored.

Commandment Six: vs. 13 "You shall not murder" shows:

F. **Love means hating to hurt.** We love to hurt those we hate, but hate to hurt those we love. My son and I were training a balky horse. When we tried to make her move, she'd rear up, throw herself backwards and land on the rider. I promised my boy I'd hold her bridle so she couldn't rear back. Trusting me, he climbed into the saddle. Unfortunately, I was no match for her. Over she went, right on top of him. He wasn't seriously hurt, but I was. It pains us when we cause hurt to someone we love.

Commandment Seven: vs. 14 "You shall not commit adultery" shows:

G. **Love means treating opposite sex as persons to be loved—not things to be used.** God says sex is part of His plan, a physical manifestation of total, permanent commitment. In that kind of love setting it's beautiful. In any other setting it's hurtful.

Commandment Eight: vs. 15 "You shall not steal" shows:

H. **Love means respecting others' property.** The preacher preached on the eighth commandment. Next day, he got on a bus to go downtown. Making his way to a seat in the back, he counted the change given him by the driver. There was a dime too much. He was tempted to just put it in his pocket. It was a long way to the front, the driver might resent being reminded of a mistake, besides the bus company would never miss it anyway. But, no, it wouldn't be right. Making his way up the long aisle, he spoke to the driver, "Excuse me, but I think you gave me too much change." "Yes, I know, 10 cents too much. I was in church yesterday and heard your sermon and decided if you didn't return it I'd never go back." Someone is watching the business transactions of every known Christian, wondering whether we really do have a special respect for the property of others.

Commandment Nine: vs. 16 "You shall not give false testimony" shows:

I. **Love means a tamed tongue.** Only love tames the tongue. Jesus said, "out of the overflow of the heart the mouth speaks" (Matt. 12:34). The tongue is fastened and controlled, not out on the tip, but down at the inside end. Pick a pig out of the barnyard, take it in the house and give it a thorough bath, spray on some cologne and tie a ribbon around its neck. Now you have a respectable pig. But forget to shut the door and out he goes— right back to pig wallow. Why? Because he's a pig and pig's enjoy filth. The only way he could be separated from filth would be for him to be born as something other than a pig. Fallen human nature has a lot of pig in it. We enjoy filth. Trying to clean ourselves up doesn't really work. We've got to let the love of Christ take over. We must be born again.

Commandment Ten: vs. 17 "You shall not covet . . . anything that belongs to your neighbor" shows:

J.   **Love means a positive attitude.** It means loving our neighbors rather than what they have—not only what they own, but their looks, brain, or spouse. Love means an appreciative attitude toward what we have rather than a covetous attitude toward what we haven't.

Conclusion

Every commandment in God's law applies love to life. Our choice is never between Christ **or** the commandments. He said, "If you love me, keep my commandments." We can't keep them without loving Him, and we can't love Him without wanting to keep them.

If we love Him, we'll love the law because he gives it to us. Two women stand chatting on the front lawn. The daughter of one comes skipping home, pops open her lunch pail and proudly produces her latest work of art. It's a paper plate to which she has glued squash seeds to produce what is supposed to be a face. But it's smeared with glue, smudged with fingerprints and creased down the middle where she had to fold it to get it into her pail. The neighbor lady turns her face and snickers. But not the mother. She accepts the gift appreciatively, presses out the crease, marches into her kitchen and places it right in the center of the refrigerator door. Now, what's the difference between those two women? That one loved art and the other didn't? Oh no, it's that one loved the artist and the other didn't.

To love the giver is to love the gift. Won't you open your heart in love for Jesus? Then you'll *want* to keep His 10 commandments. To love *Him* is to love *them*. To love the giver is to love the gift.

506. *Ishi*

[Exemplifies two sermon types in one sermon. It's basically an expository sermon on the book of Hosea, but division four is totally narrative and exercises considerable imagination. Easily adapted to youth. Topic: God's unending love.]

Introduction

As surely as Christ has a personalized plan for getting each of us saved in heaven, Satan has a custom made plan for getting us lost in hell. His favorite is to give us a wrong idea of what God is like, because he knows better than anyone that if we knew what God is really like we'd love Him.

Everyone has a picture of God. Typically, it comes from our father. If Dad was permissive, we may assume God is indifferent to obedience. If we could manipulate him to get our own way, we'll try it with God also. If father was busy, or demanding, or rejecting and impossible to please, or absent when we needed Him we subconsciously tend to presume our Heavenly Father is the same way. Be patient with those who can't love God. If you had their picture of what He's like you probably couldn't love Him either. But if our picture is wrong, our Christian experience suffers. We must get rid of that false god before we can love the true God.

Hosea 2:16 gives two opposing pictures people have of God. Some see Him as "Baali" (KJV), oppressing master, stern authority. But God is really "Ishi"—husband, lover. Let's learn about *Ishi*, the lover God, from the fascinating book of Hosea, because:

Theme: *To understand God's love is to love God.*

We'll notice three things Hosea says about God's love, then close with a love story.

I. **God's love is unending.**
There's nothing you can ever do to make God stop loving you. Now, you can make Him stop saving you. Just stop loving and serving Him.
   A. **Our goodness and love terribly temporary**—Hosea 6:4. Our love for God no more lasting than morning fog or summer dew. We renew our commitment to Christ Sabbath morning, but it hardly lasts till dinner is over, much less all week.
   B. **God loves us even when we wander**—Hosea 14:4a "heal." Doing carpenter work I reached into my nail pouch and cut my finger on the utility knife I forgot was there. I put the knife in the other pocket so it wouldn't happen again. But I forgot that too. Just a few minutes later I reached my other hand into that pocket and cut myself a second time. I felt a fool, but also experienced a miracle. Very soon the bleeding stopped. In a few minutes the pain went away. Not many days later the cut was filled in with new skin and I eventually forgot even which fingers were cut. That was God at work. God is a miraculous healer of even our most foolish hurts.

   "Love them freely," vs 4b. Abundantly, unreservedly. The little girl was reprimanding her younger brother for being naughty. Shaking her finger, she declared, "If you do that, Daddy won't love you anymore." But father overheard. Pulling both onto his lap he explained, "That really isn't quite right. When you're good I love you with a heart that's happy. When you're not, I love you with a heart that's sad. But don't ever forget, I'll always love you, good or bad." That's the way God loves and the way his people ought to love. Every church member has a right to expect there'll be someone in the congregation godlike enough to love them freely—good or bad.

II. God's love is aggressive.

Hosea 2:14 "desert" God sometimes has to pull us off life's freeway where the noise is so loud we can't hear the still small voice. Next time you feel the heat of a trial that comes your way, remember He allows desert experiences only to have you alone so He can get through to you.

"Allure her" God is an active lover. He doesn't just wait for us to come to Him. He pursues, allures us. The small son of a friend of ours looked at Sallman's painting of Christ, with the long, flowing hair and soft eyes. Turning to his father, he asked, "Is Jesus a girl?" Men and youth sometimes have trouble identifying with a Christ and Christianity which seem to them effeminate. But God's love is not like the girl who gets herself prettied up then passively waits for a lover to come. God's love is aggressive like the 12-year-old boy I watched at campmeeting. It was obvious he was fascinated by a girl about his age. He pulled her hair, he chased her around the building. He ran ahead of her to the door, and I hoped for a moment his manners had improved when he opened the door for her—only to see him slam it in her face! A young man may do something stupid in trying to impress his beloved, but he'll do something. His love is aggressive. And so is God's.

III. God's love is dedicated to our success.

A. God downgrades our failures, delights in our successes.

Hosea 11:3a "taking them by the arms." Hosea's illustration is a familiar one. You've been there when father and mother announce to the world that their wee one has started walking. Maybe it's a family get-together. Grandma sucks in her breath at the announcement, "He's already walking at 11 months?" "Sure, watch." Mother sets him down on his rubbery legs and, holding him under his arms, half hands him over to Dad. "See, he can walk." They get a little farther apart and try it again. Eventually, the inevitable. Down he goes. Now what does father do? Kick him in the corner, "Dumb kid, make a fool out of me in front of the whole family?" Never. He reaches down and grabs his son under the arms and pops him back onto his feet, hopefully before anyone even notices the fall. That's Hosea's illustration. That's how God wants to handle our failures.

B. God sees us, not as we are, but as we could become. They say Michelangelo could look at a shapeless slab of marble and see an angel waiting to emerge. How can we help but love the God who sees the good in us and wants to make something beautiful of us?

IV. God's love exemplified.

I want to share a love story that dramatically illustrates how God loves. It's an almost unbelievable, yet true story, from an unimpeachable source. I'll admit to imagining some of the details, but the story is based on fact.

It seems this young preacher fell deeply in love with a young woman. I'd like to think she was beautiful. I know he thought she was. In due course, they married and their love produced a bouncing baby boy. The husband dearly loved both wife and son. He was content. But his wife was not. One day he came home to find a note, "Baby next door. Be back later." He put his little boy to bed and waited up for his wife, who didn't get home till the wee hours of the morning.

One day he came home to a house that looked like a cyclone had hit. He cleaned up the kitchen and went looking for his wife. And he found her in a tavern, laughing and carrying on with the men at the bar—a preacher's wife. Soon their second child was born, a little girl. Maybe his wife could be content now. But no, the escapades continued. Sadly, the new baby was given a name meaning "not loved."

Another time he came home to find his wife had left the children all alone. Baby was in her crib and the little boy in his playpen. He'd cried himself hoarse. Husband found someone to care for the kids and went looking for his wandering wife. And he found her—in the red light district. By now they were no longer living as husband and wife, yet she became pregnant a third time. In total humiliation, yet with undying love, he took some other man's son into his family. This baby's name meant "not my people."

Then his wife left home for good. He thought he knew all the haunts and dives in town, but try as he might he couldn't find her. Night after night he sat rocking the baby till his arms ached like his heart ached. For he still loved his wandering wife.

Finally, he found her. He hardly recognized her at first. Her face was pale, hair stringy, eyes bloodshot. She was dirty and diseased and she smelled of cheap perfume. She had gotten into debt and, as was the custom in this country, was being sold into slavery in lieu of payment. The auctioneer yanked off what few clothes covered her. Bidders had a right to see what they were getting. But her naked body was bony and emaciated. The bidding began. Nobody wanted her very badly. But her husband did. He bid 15 pieces of silver, but it wasn't enough. Desperately, he pushed his way to the front. He had found her and simply couldn't lose her again. "I have 10 bushels of barley to see us through the winter. I bid 15 pieces of silver and 10 bushels of barley. It's everything I have." The gavel fell and she was his.

Slipping his arm around her he took her home, bathed her emaciated body, prepared food, then helped her into bed where she fell into a fitful sleep. As he sat beside her in the twilight the tears came. But those tears became telescopes that helped him see a bigger picture. As preachers will, his mind began to form a sermon. A sermon about how God hurts when we wander, how much He loves us still and how desperately He wants us back.

God said, "Put it in the book," and the story has come down to us through 2800 years as the first three chapters of the book of Hosea. The story of Hosea the faithful husband and Gomer the wandering wife. An illustration of God's love for us and how He wants us back.

Conclusion

God's love is unending, aggressive, dedicated to our success. Who could be so selfish as to presume on a love like that? God wants you back, today. If some sin has come between, He wants you back. If you've dragged His name in the dirt, He wants you back. If you've wandered away, He wants you back. Doesn't your heart respond to a love like that? Won't you come back? To understand God's love is to love God.

507. God's Westminster Abbey

[Expository-topical sermon. Division I is expository. Divisions II and III are topical. Topic: Christian growth. Moves progressively from negative to positive.]

Introduction

London's Westminster Abbey is a grand cathedral where England buries her honored dead. As I walked its aisles I saw, beneath the floors and behind the walls, inscriptions identifying the tombs of dead heroes. What kinds of people does England honor most? I noted kings, statesmen, scholars, soldiers.

God too has a Westminster Abbey—Hebrews 11. There lie buried those whom God honors most. As we walk its aisles, we're in for some surprises, for:

Theme: *With God it's not what been, but what becoming that counts.*

I. God honors some unusual people.
A. God honors:
Abel (vs. 4). God honors martyrs. That's good.
Enoch (vs. 5). God honors those who walk with Him. That's good.
Noah (vs. 7). God honors those who preach righteousness. That's good. But wait a minute! Didn't Noah celebrate after the flood by getting drunk (Gen. 9)? You mean God honors preachers who get drunk occasionally?

And what about *Rahab* (vs. 31) the prostitute? Does God honor women who sell their bodies?

B. God especially honors:

Abraham (vs. 8). There's an 8 foot inscription over his grave in God's Westminster Abbey—8 verses about Abraham. But Abraham was a liar. He told officials Sara was his sister rather than his wife. And he did it repeatedly (Gen. 12, 20). It was a clever lie. Brothers of women coveted by the potentate got gifts. Husbands got killed. And when the rulers threw him out as an undesirable alien, what did God do? He took him in and gave him a special place in God's Westminster Abbey.

Moses (vs. 24). There's a 7 foot inscription over Moses' grave— 7 verses about Moses in Hebrews 11. But Moses was a murderer (Ex. 2). Today, we'd call him a cop killer. One whom God honors most.

David (vs. 32). He was both an adulterer and a murderer. He was also a "peeping Tom" (2 Sam. 11). The amazing thing is that all this happened while he was president of the General Conference. You've heard of leaders making mistakes, but surely none greater than David's. One whom God honors most.

Whatever is the lesson? That God is not particular? No:

C. God rewards growth —vs. 33, 34b "whose weakness was turned to strength." With God it's not what we've been, but what we're becoming that counts.

This brings comfort to the guilty. With God, it's not what we've done, but what we're doing; not where we've been, but where we're going; not how tall we are, but how much we're growing.

This brings warning to the complacent. One time conversion is not enough. When our second son was born, he was given the crib and our two-year-old was given a regular bed. Ellen and I had an agreement about night duty. If the baby cried she'd go. If it was our eldest it was my job. I thought I'd made a wonderful bargain, but was not as smart as I thought. Terry, unused to a bed without sides, kept falling out. One night I heard a thump followed by a whimper. Dutifully I responded. There he was, in a heap on the floor. I tucked him into his bed and went back to sleep. Another thump. Again I put him back to bed. This time my head no more than hit the pillow, when out he went again. I helped him up and tried to waken him enough to help him understand this was not the proper procedure. "Son, why do you keep falling out of bed?" Only half awake, he rubbed his eyes and answered, "I guess I stayed too close to where I got in."

Christian, have you stayed too close to where you got in? Perhaps there is a sin that used to bother you. You still have the sin, it just doesn't bother you anymore. Are you spending less time in prayer and Bible study? Are your personal standards lowering? Is your relationship with Christ drifting? With God it's not what you've been, but what you're becoming that counts.

II. **God honors overcomers**—Rev. 3:21.
   A. **David overcame**. When Nathan the prophet reminded him of his sin, David sat down and wrote Psalm 51, "Cleanse me with hyssop," "Create in me a pure heart." Shame on David for being such a big sinner, but because he was an even bigger repenter, he became one of the biggest overcomers. Those who sin timidly tend to repent halfheartedly.
   B. **Moses overcame**. His problems were pride and temper. But he became the meekest man on earth (Num. 12:3).
   C. **Abraham overcame**. He and God were still working on Abraham's growth at age 99 (Gen. 17). He's a special model for us as we grow older and the concrete tends to set. We must never credit ourselves with overcoming sins we've grown too old to enjoy. We drop off sin after sin as we lose the energy to commit them—and call it growth. But we're still as self-centered, stubborn, unloving as ever, and wondering why our kids and grandkids aren't attracted to our beliefs. Abraham was still growing at 99.
   D. **Heaven to overcomers**—Revelation mentions often: Rev. 2:7, 3:5. Rev. 3:12a "make a pillar in the temple." A building is dependent on, held up by pillars. Heaven will be dependent on, held up by overcomers. If God brought to heaven only people who had always been good, the angels would yawn. The omnipotence of God is best proven by His making bad people fit for heaven. Great sinners who have become greater overcomers are the greatest proof of the power of Christ. And when He gets Floyd Bresee to heaven, the whole universe will know there's power in the Blood.
   E. **With Christ overcomers come first.** Why did Jesus appear first to Mary Magdalene after His resurrection? I would never have done it that way. I'd have gone to *Caesar*, raised my fist, and shouted, "Your seal was worthless, your army powerless." Or pointed my finger at *Caiaphas*, "Your plot has backfired. More will follow me now than ever." Or hurried to *mother Mary*, "Don't cry, Mother, I'm alive." Why first to former prostitute? Perhaps to show us that, with the risen Lord, overcomers come first.

III. **How to be an overcomer**—Three steps:
   A. **See your sins in the light of the cross.** It's unlikely we'll ever overcome sins of which we're unaware. We're tempted to see our sins in *comparison* with the sins of others. For example, sexual purity.

Our standards are invariably higher than the world's. Yet, as the world's standards lower, ours tend to still stay about the same distance above, so that if the world's standards get low enough our standards become lower than the world's used to be. Perhaps the worst condemnation of Christianity is that our standards tend to reflect the standards of society more than of the Scripture which we claim to follow.

B. **Rely on Christ's Power.** Phil. 4:13. We should be a "can do" people. It's true there are powerful temptations *out there*, but we've a more powerful Savior *up there.*

C. **Feed spiritual nature.** Babies can't grow on one meal a week, Christians can't grow on spiritual food just on Sabbath. Spiritual growth demands that we find some effective way to feed the spiritual nature daily.

Conclusion

With God it's not what we've been, but what we're becoming that counts. Let's not worry about what we've been, but let's not be satisfied with what we are. Those God honors most were not good all their lives. Rather, they struggled with sin all their lives until, through Christ, they overcame. Let's see our sins, not in comparison with others, but in light of the cross; rely on Christ's power to overcome them and resolve to feed our spiritual nature daily.

Pretend we have two dogs living across the fence from one another—one named Nice and the other named Nasty. Now, Nice and Nasty don't like each other one bit. One day, they dig under the fence and start to fight. They're an even match. For a while Nasty is on top and Nice on the bottom. Then it's Nasty on the bottom and Nice on top. Neither can win. Their owners pull them apart and patch the fence. Then an awful thing happens, Nice's family goes on vacation and the boy who was supposed to feed him forgets—Nice gets nothing but water. Meanwhile, Nasty is getting balanced meals every single day. At the end of two weeks the dogs come together again. Nice can hardly stand up, but still he fights. Now, which dog will win? The dog you feed is the dog that wins.

We each have two dogs fighting in our backyard every day. Paul calls them our carnal and spiritual natures. Which will win the battle for your soul? Too many of us feed Nasty all week and pray for Nice to win. It won't work. The dog you feed is the dog that wins.

508. Why a Church?

[Topical sermon. This sermon and 509 exemplify a short sermon series.

Series topic: church. Sermon topic: purpose of church. Example of extensive use of illustration. Note the contrasting use of negative and positive in division II.]

Introduction

The US Congress gloated when a survey showed the confidence of American voters in their President was at an all time low. But pride turned to chagrin when second survey showed confidence in Congress was lower still. Modern society emphasizes independence and individual freedom. Institutions and organizations are suspect. Who would have dared to criticize the FBI or CIA a generation ago? Who would dare defend them now?

The church is an organization. When society is suspicious of organizations there's a special temptation to ask, Why a church? You can worship at home, pay your tithe where you please or just spend your money on yourself. We see mistakes among church leaders, too much hypocrisy among church members. No wonder we ask, Why a church?

Love is learned behavior. We're born with a need for love and a potential for love, but we're not born loving. God provides an institution called the home where, surrounded by loving mother and father, sister and brother, the baby learns to love. When we're born again as Christians we're not born totally loving. So again, God provides an institution where, surrounded by love, we learn to love. That's why a church.

Theme: *Surrounded by love we learn to love, surrounded by loving*
            Christians we learn to love Christ.

   I. **The church is God's idea.**
      A. **God uses organization.** Acts 2:47b "the Lord added". The idea of adding people to the church is the Lord's idea. And whom does He add? "Those who were being saved." There is then, some relationship between salvation and church membership. The one's He's saving He wants in His organization, the church.

         Our God is a great organizer. Look down through a microscope until your eye focuses on a single cell, and what do you see? Precise, predictable organization. Look up through a telescope pointed anyplace in the universe, and what do you see? Precise, predictable organization. Anyplace God is at work we see organization. Then if He is at work saving souls we would naturally expect Him to use an organization, His church.

      B. **God's organizations work.** The church today is like the ark in Noah's day. The ark was undoubtedly an imperfect boat because it was built by a human being—and him a preacher. But when the flood came it did the job of helping God save His people, for it was made after

God's plan. The church is an imperfect organization because it's made up of human beings, but it'll do the job of helping God save His people, for it's made after God's plan.

I have the privilege of being married to a very lovely lady. Sometimes I have felt, however, that my Ellen has a super sensitive nose. It tends to twitch violently when we go by a Colorado feedlot or an Iowa pig farm. Did you ever think of what a problem Mrs. Noah had if hers was a nose like that? They didn't housebreak those animals before they came into the ark, and I understand the ventilation was none too good. I've sometimes thought Mrs. Noah might never have stood the stench in the ark if it were not for the storm outside.

We must apologize for any imperfection inside the church, but really, it's nothing compared to the ugliness outside. The potential curse of a second or third generation Adventist is that, having spent our whole lifetime inside the ark, we think it's the only place that smells. That's why evangelism is the lifeblood of the church. Every congregation needs people continuously coming in out of the storm to remind them of how much nicer it is in here than out there.

C. **Christ loves the church as a bride.** 2 Cor. 11:2. In Eden *Adam* slept, his side was opened and Eve emerged. At Calvary the *second Adam* slept, His side was opened and the church emerged. As Eve stood before Adam in Eden, how he loved her. As the church stands before Christ today, how He loves her. Be cautious about criticizing the church. You're criticizing Christ's bride. And no good man takes it lightly when you criticize his bride, even if she deserves it.

D. **A Christian is one who loves Christ and wants to do as Christ did.** Our eldest son was about two when we visited his grandparents on a hot summer day. We gathered in the backyard where the lawn sprinkler was turning. Terry had on his bathing suit, Grandpa, his old clothes. Grandad thought it would be great fun to tease the little boy into running through the sprinkler. "Get right behind me." Grandpa headed for the sprinkler, but not really wanting to get wet himself, turned aside at the last moment, hoping Terry would run right through. It didn't work. When Grandpa turned, Terry turned. "Get real close and run real fast." Grandpa ran a little closer to the sprinkler and turned the sharpest corner he could at the very last second. But the boy could out-turn his Grandad any day. Nothing worked but for Grandpa to run right through the sprinkler. The little boy gladly followed.

Isn't that the way it ought to be between Christ and the Christian? Where He turns away, we turn. Where He leads, we follow. Then we can easily settle the issue of church membership.

All we have to do is find out what Jesus did and we'll want to do it too. Ephesians 5:25 tells us two things Jesus did about the church.

First, "Christ *loved* the church." Change the church, improve the church, but first love the church. Sometimes we love power, control and getting our own way more than we love church.

Second, He "*gave himself* up for her." When give ourselves, time, talent, money for the church we're being Christlike.

II. **What is a church? What is its purpose?**

A. **A church is not a building**. In the first century after Christ some think there were as many as five million converts to Christianity. But we can't find a single building. On the other hand, during the Dark Ages when the church was least successful, it built the most lavish buildings.

B. **A church is not a group of perfect people.** The church must have standards for church membership, higher standards for church leadership, but no standards for church fellowship or friendship. If sinners don't feel at home in your church it's not a Christian church no matter what the sign says, for those who felt themselves sinners always felt at home around Christ.

We are the church. The church may not be what we want it to be, but it will be what we are. If we want Christ-centered, loving, live, enthusiastic church it can happen only if we are that kind of church member. And we should each praise the Lord hypocrites are allowed in the church, else where would **we** join? All of us are less on the inside than we pretend to be on the outside. In ourselves we call it "room for growth." In others we call it hypocrisy.

C. **A church is not formed as a hierarchy**, not first and second class citizens, Matt. 23:8-11. The relationship between the people and their leaders in the church is not to be that of masters and servants, but of brothers and sisters. Professionalism has always been the curse of the church. When the church has been run by clergy it has always run downhill. How are churches taken over by the professionals? It happens when members are too lukewarm to be willing to do the work of the church, barely interested enough to pay somebody else to do it.

These are some of the things a church is not. Now two things a church is:

D. **A church is a group working together** *to help others love Christ.* 1 Cor. 12:25, 26. As a boy, I went barefoot in the summer. And I was forever stubbing my toe. Usually the big one. And it hurt, especially if I had stubbed the same toe the day before. But I learned a great theology from it, for every time I really stubbed my toe, my stomach got upset. Now, it's a long way from toe to tummy even on a little boy, but that's the way the body works. When one part hurts the rest of the body hurts too. And Paul says the church is meant to work like the body.

E. **A church is a place for healing the hurts of life.** I used to visit a hospital where the nursing station in the emergency area had a sign on the glass. In the shape and color of a stop sign, it declared, "The pain stops here." Good motto for a hospital. Good motto for a church. Could we honestly put it on the front of our pulpits, "The pain stops here?"

One day my wife fell down the basement stairs at home. She ended her fall with her arm slamming against the concrete wall at the bottom of the stairs. A bone in her wrist broke and came right through the skin. The pain was excruciating. We got her into the car and raced for the hospital as I kept seeing that sign, "The pain stops here." Everything would be all right if I could just get her to the hospital. As we drove into the emergency area a nurse came rushing out. Medication was soon applied and the hospital kept its word, the pain began to go away.

And we learned something some church members never seem to quite comprehend. Ellen had to stay in the hospital for several days. But all the time she was there not once did any doctor, nurse, aid or orderly scold her for falling down the stairs. Frankly, we knew before we ever got there that falling down the stairs was not a good idea.

When sinners fall down and make a mess of their lives, church members sometimes seem to feel it their duty to scold them for falling down. Chances are they already knew that falling down was not a good idea. What they need from the church is *hope* that, through Christ, they can stand again. Less scolding and more *healing.*

Hospitals are expensive, yet people keep right on going, because they stop pain. And *nobody stops going anywhere that stops their pain.* What is a church backslider? We sometimes define backsliders as worldly, undependable. Let me suggest another definition. A backslider is simply someone whose pain the church has failed to stop. For nobody stops going anywhere that stops their pain.

Conclusion

So we've learned that the church is God's idea. An organization He's designed for teaching us to love. Surrounded by love we learn to love, surrounded by loving Christians we learn to love Christ.

Some African herds have the instinct to form a big circle when the lion is on the prowl. Inside the circle is a smaller circle made up of the very young, the very old, the very sick, the very weak, the very ones the lion is after. But those in the outer circle, horns pointed out, form an impenetrable fortress as they offer themselves in protection of those the lion would devour.

I leave you with that picture of the church. The Bible says "the devil prowls around like a roaring lion looking for someone to devour" (1 Pet 5:8). I challenge you to be strong enough to volunteer for duty in the outer circle, providing the loving support of the church to those who are weak. I encourage you to be humble enough to sometimes realize you need to be in the inner circle and receive loving support from the church. Above all else, I invite you to stay in the circle. Help the church become all Christ intended it to be. A place where, surrounded by loving Christians, we learn to love Christ.

509. Lay Lib

[Topical sermon. This sermon and sermon 508 exemplify a short sermon series. Series topic: church. Sermon topic: spiritual gifts in the church. Introduction exemplifies use of statistics.

Notice that little summary is needed in the conclusion. The summary is actually in the closing illustration.]

Introduction
Exciting news! The SDA church is growing as never before. Between 1982 and 1985 we baptized 1 million souls in 3 years; 85-90, 2 million in 5 years; 90-95, 3 million in 5 years; 95-2000, praying for 4 million in 5 years. During the short years of my ministry we grew from 700,000 to 8 million.

We're growing fastest outside America where movement began. Visiting Papua New Guinea, I asked the union president how many churches he had. "I don't know." I asked mission president. "I don't know." I asked district pastor. "I don't know. I have so many churches and get around so seldom that every time I visit, my members have started more churches."

How could my congregation grow like that? How can we finish the work where we are? A friend of mine noticed a stamp machine in a post office lobby, with a sign that read, "If everything else fails, read the directions." Apparently people had put their money in the machine and no stamps came out. They probably criticized, cursed and kicked it. Did everything but read the directions. Church members sometimes feel they put their time and money into the church but nothing happens, no growth results. They complain, they criticize, do everything but read the directions. Today, we're going to quit complaining and try looking at the New Testament directions for a successful church. And what the directions are going to tell us is that the church is in dire need of a strong "lay liberation" movement. Where churches grow fastest, there are fewer pastors and more working members, a mutual ministry between pastor and people. The directions say:

Theme: *Everyone receiving Holy Spirit receives ministering gift.*

I. **Every member a minister.**
Every member ministry doesn't mean that every member is a preacher. If being a minister frightens you, hold on a few minutes for some good news.

   A. **In the early church little separation between laity and clergy.** The original word for laity is *laos*, for clergy *kleros*. As we study the use of these two words in New Testament and New Testament times we see them used quite interchangeably. The church was seen as a community of ministers. Under this plan the gospel spread like wildfire.

   B. **Devil's plan to stall church: separation.** The devil was deeply disturbed. He introduced a new plan: The clergy would study Bible, teach, do work of church; the laity would no longer be obliged to minister, they were to be ministered to. Their only obligations were to pray, pay and obey. This diabolical plan worked. The clergy liked the prestige and power of possessing the only keys of the kingdom. The laity liked having less responsibility.

   Even church architecture of the period said separation. They put railings across the front of the church platform, separating laity and clergy. They fastened pulpits high on front walls of the sanctuary like swallow's nests, separating clergy and laity. They dressed the clergy in beautiful, long-flowing robes, very attractive but very different from the laity. And the fire went out. All down through history, when the church has been taken over by the clergy it has always grown cold.

   C. **Protestant reformation emphasized individual priesthood**—1 Peter 2:9 "Royal priesthood . . . that you may declare" or proclaim. Protestant converts liked the idea of being "priests" who could go directly to heaven for forgiveness without the offices of their clergy. But a priest's principal role is not ministering for himself, but to declare or proclaim Christ to others. This truth has been given only mental assent by most Protestants, including Adventists. It is taken seriously by only a few, such as Jehovah's Witnesses.

   Two of the fastest growing denominations in Christianity have little or no pastoral ministry as we think of it—Jehovah's Witnesses and Mormons. It seems to me both have a rather difficult doctrine. Why are they growing so profusely? Because they have the right method. Adventists have the right message, but have not made enough use of the right method. The devil isn't frightened by either message or method, but when Christ's church combines them it will finish Christ's work and seal the devil's doom.

   D. **Members are the ministry of the church.** Usually the best person to win another person is a person who sits where that person sits. The best person to win a farmer, another farmer; business person, a business person; housewife, a housewife; youth, an older youth. How many pulpits are there in a church with 100 active members: one? or 101? Don't you see what a difference it would make in the growth of a congregation if every school desk where a member taught became a pulpit, every workbench, every hospital bed, every kitchen table a pulpit?

II. Every member given gift/s.

Christ assigned His church an awesome task, taking His gospel to the whole world. Christianity would be a farce unless He provided some plan, some means by which the task could be accomplished. Here it is:

A. **Everyone receiving Holy Spirit receives gift of spirit**—Eph. 4:8,11 "gave gifts to men." Ladies often hold a bridal shower for a woman about to be married. Some sit down and work hour after hour to make something to take to the bride, others shop all over town to find just the right gift for the bride, others put some money in a pretty envelope for the bride. Notice the gifts are very diverse, yet no one would think of coming to the shower without a gift. That's how it is with the Holy Spirit. Gifts are diverse, but the Holy Spirit wouldn't think of coming into our lives without bringing one or more gifts.

To be practical, I think our gift is a spin-off of some talent we already had. But when we give ourselves to Christ, the Holy Spirit shows us how to use our gifts to perform some ministry for Christ.

B. **Pastor's principal work is preparing people to use their gifts**— Eph. 4:11c, 12a "prepare God's people for works of service." The pastor's work and the church's planning should not center around slot-filling, but people-developing. Less around programs to be perpetuated or offices to be filled and more around finding what gifts God has given members and how they can best be developed and used in the church's ministry.

C. **We choose our own ministry, but not our own gift**—1 Cor. 12:7-11 "each one" "as he (Holy Spirit) determines." Herein lies the strongest argument against undue emphasis on speaking in tongues. It is easy to prove (Acts 2) that tongues can be literal, but much harder to prove they cannot be ecstatic (1 Cor. 14). There are three principal lists of spiritual gifts (Rom. 12, 1 Cor 12, Eph 4). For the sake of illustration, we'll say there are about 20 spiritual gifts. One of the 20 is tongues.

The charismatic is right in insisting that everyone receiving the Holy Spirit receives a spiritual gift. But wrong when insisting it must be the gift of tongues. The Holy Spirit, not any person or denomination determines which gift the individual receives. But the charismatic is no more wrong in presuming the gift must be tongues than we would be in presuming we have no gift at all. To say we have no gift would be to say we have no Holy Spirit, for everyone receiving the Holy Spirit receives a spiritual gift.

    D. **Never belittle a gift that isn't yours**—1 Cor. 12:1,4. Christ has great confidence in His church. Otherwise He would not have done such a dangerously divisive thing as placing different gifts in the same congregation. It's only having the same Spirit that keeps us united in spite of our differing gifts.

        It's only natural that others' gifts seem less important to me than mine. This chapter likens the church to a body. Imagine with me a man waking up one morning and starting to put on his glasses. He can't see a thing without them. Just as he's about to settle his glasses on his nose, the nose speaks up, "Hold it. No glasses on this nose. I used to look fairly nice, but see those red blotches on either side of me? Glasses have made a mess of me. If the eyes want glasses, let the eyes hold them. No glasses on this nose!" The man has no choice but to put his glasses back on the nightstand. Getting up, he starts across the room, bumps into the open door and bends his nose. You see, it's true the eyes needed the nose, but equally true that the nose needed the eyes. And so in the church. Every gift the Spirit brings a given congregation is necessary. Every gift needs the others if all the work God wants done is to get done.

        Many church problems stem from favoring our gifts and failing to appreciate the gifts of others. If we have the gift of helps, we believe the church should concentrate on welfare work, community centers, ADRA. If our gift is healing, the way to finish the work is through health evangelism, hospitals, clinics, better living centers. Much of our criticism of conference and pastor is because we insist on the preeminence of our own gift. Thankfully, one of the spiritual gifts is wisdom. Those with that gift should be on our committees to find ways to support all the gifts.

        Now, I promised good news to those fearful of being ministers.

III. **We're responsible only for gifts God gives us**—1 Peter 4:10a.

    A. **Everyone does something, not everyone does the same thing.** Christ never asks you to minister by means of a gift you don't have. Shame on pastors who make members feel guilty for failing to exercise the pastor's gift.

    B. **You'll enjoy using your own gift.** If you haven't been enjoying witnessing, you've probably been trying to do it by means of a gift you don't have. That's why you fail. And that's why you don't want to do it again. It's not that we don't want to witness. It's that we don't want to fail again. But when we witness by means of a gift we have, we tend to succeed. And when we succeed we enjoy doing it again.

Conclusion

The church is like an orchestra. Each member of a good orchestra is a *gifted* musician. Each member of the congregation should be gifted. Everyone should have received the Holy Spirit who always brings gifts. The orchestra's gifts are as *different* as the violinist is from the drummer. The church's gifts are as different as teaching is from hospitality. The orchestra conductor doesn't make the music, but *inspires and coordinates* each member in playing their own instruments. The church pastor's work is not to do the members' work but inspire them by preaching, and coordinate their work by careful planning and effective training.

God has placed in your congregation every gift needed to do the work He wants done. The Holy Spirit is waiting right now to help **you** find and use your spiritual gift. Both you and your church will prosper so long as members join their gifts together in mutual ministry. Success. Guaranteed.

510. Your Second Job

[Textual sermon from Acts 1:8. Topic: Christian service. Example of a sermon with many divisions and few subdivisions. Conclusion closes with the sermon text.]

Introduction

It was Albert Schweitzer who so emphatically insisted that, to feel fulfilled, every Christian needs a second job. Our first job is to make a *living*. Our second is to make a *life*.

Our second job is one for which we receive no pay in money. It's purpose is purely to meet the needs of others. Yet the pay is big, because it relieves our stress. It decreases boredom by giving us a change of pace and by unleashing our creativity. It leaves us feeling good, for it rescues us from drowning in our own self-centeredness.

(Acts 1:9) tells the story of Jesus ascension after His death, burial and resurrection. We tend to treasure the last words of our loved ones. Here are the last words of Jesus—Acts 1:8. Let's hold a magnifying glass up to these famous last words. They tell us about our second job. Jesus is saying:

Theme: *We are saved to serve.*

I. **Personal experience precedes our service.**

Acts 1:8b "you will be my *witnesses*" A lot of us would rather be *lawyers* than witnesses. Lawyers argue the fine points of law, persuading people by the force of their arguments. Witnesses have experienced something and simply tell what's happened to them. Christ wants us to change people by sharing the change our Christian experience has made in us. If your hands were horribly disfigured and you found a doctor who corrected your problem you wouldn't need some special training or great gift to convince other disfigured people to go to your doctor. You'd simply show them your hands.

II. **Christ is focus of our service.**

Acts 1:8b "you will be *my* witnesses. The purpose of Christian witness is not to show we are good, or even that our church is good, but that Christ is good. The principal purpose of Christian witness is **Christian** witness, not just sociological improvement. We feed the hungry, not just so they can go to hell with full stomachs, but so they learn that the Christ who cares about their hunger, can be trusted when He says, "I am the resurrection and the life. He who believes in me will live, even though he dies" (John 11:25).

The little boy was intently working his crayon across the paper when the Bible school teacher bent over him asking, "What are you drawing?" "I'm drawing a picture of God." "But nobody knows what God looks like." "They'll know when I get through." The purpose of Christian service is so people will know what God is like when we get through.

III. **Holy Spirit empowers our service.**

A. **Holy Spirit brings power**—vs. 8a "you will receive power when the Holy Spirit comes." The word "power" comes from the Greek word *dunamis* from which we get our word dynamite. With the Holy Spirit comes explosive, dynamite power. Power to move the world.

B. **Holy Spirit brings gifts**—vs. 8b "when the Holy Spirit comes . . . you will be my witnesses." Why must the Holy Spirit precede witnessing? One reason is the Holy Spirit brings to each individual a spiritual gift or gifts for witnessing. To say we have no gift for service would be to say we have no Holy Spirit. This spiritual gift is probably a spin-off of some talent we already had, but the Holy Spirit suggests ways to use it in ministering to others for Christ.

C. **Holy Spirit protects us from selfish service**—vs. 8a "when the Holy Spirit comes **on** you." The sociologist says even Christians serve for selfish reasons: to be important, praised or loved. Worst of all, possibly to control. Love that leads to selfless service cannot be conjured up from within. It must be sent down from above.

Now Jesus draws four concentric circles:

IV. **First circle—home service**—vs. 8b "you will be my witnesses in *Jerusalem.*" We could interpret this to mean our local city, but since Jesus is referring to the circle closest to us, it would seem proper to translate it as the family circle. Some of us get so busy serving church and community that we neglect service at home. Father was hurrying off to what he no doubt perceived to be some important service. Dashing out of the house and heading for the car in the driveway, he noticed his son standing on the lawn with a ball glove on one hand and a ball in the other. Meaning to be a good father, he detoured by way of his boy, patted him on the head and said, "I love you, son." "Aw, Dad, I don't want you to love me. I want you to play ball with me." When we have time for serving everyone but our own family they've a right to question our love for them.

V. **Second circle—community service**—vs. 8b "you will be my witnesses . . . in all *Judea*." The next nearest circle of service would take in our neighborhood and local church. A ship came limping in from a long and difficult sea voyage and anchored beyond the mouth of a river. Immediately the captain signaled the shore, "Send fresh water." Back came the reply, "Drop your buckets." Knowing it was impossible to drink sea water, the captain felt someone was playing a foolish joke. Twice more he sent the same request. Twice more came the same reply. Finally, he decided the reply might be a serious one. Lowering a bucket, he learned the river current carried clear out to sea. He was surrounded by fresh, salt-free water .

We sometimes presume places to serve are far beyond our reach. Actually, we're surrounded by service opportunities wherever we are. There's someone who works next to us, lives next to us, worships next to us who has a need we could meet if we really cared.

VI. **Third circle—cross-cultural service**—vs. 8b "you will be my witnesses . . . in *Samaria*." The race barrier between Jew and Samaritan in Jesus day was probably as bad or worse than any existing today. Jesus said Christian service is to cross such barriers. God created only one Adam so no one could ever say, "My ancestry is better than yours." We all came from a single source.

Social scientists bring both bad and good news about Christian prejudice. The bad news is that research indicates churchgoers tend to be more prejudiced than nonchurchgoers. Why? When we feel our group comprises God's chosen, then those outside our group are the unchosen and are to be separated from for fear of contamination or compromise. The good news is that highly active churchgoers tend to be less prejudiced than nonchurchgoers. Those who take Christianity most seriously come to realize that we are all one—that prejudice isn't Christian.

VII. **Fourth circle—international service**—vs. 8b "you will be my witnesses . . . to the *ends of the earth*." The SDA church has the largest Protestant mission organization in the world. World population is growing about 2% per year, Protestant membership also 2%, SDA membership 7%. It took 111 years for SDAs to reach one million membership. We are baptizing nearly one million every year now. However, a decline in mission emphasis and giving in North America could place the future of our mission program in jeopardy.

Conclusion

We are saved to serve. Movement and momentum are as essential in the Adventist church as in riding a bicycle. If we stop moving we'll fall. The same is true of our personal spirituality. You need a second job, purposely chosen to fit your gifts, interests and surroundings. Determine to find it today. It's not just a good idea, it's our divine commission from Jesus famous last words—Acts 1:8.

511. The Good Shepherd

[Expository sermon outline on a psalm—Psalm 23. Topic: dependence.]

Introduction

Jesus called us sheep. Not flattering. Why sheep? Illustrate our need of depending on Good Shepherd.

Theme: *You can depend on the Good Shepherd.*

Four rewards complete dependence:
   I. **Removes need for fear**—Psalm 23:1, 2.
      A. **Shepherd understands and removes need for *sheep's* fear.** Sheep fear water. Hard to swim in wool overcoat. Shepherd creates little pool of still water .
      B. **Good shepherd understands and removes need for *our* fear.** Everybody afraid of something—unattractive, unloved, lonely, sickness, death.
   II. **His way pays**—vs. 3
      Sheep paths invariably led uphill from the sheepfold. Harder path, but led to where grass grew in coolness of higher altitude. If not climbing not going anywhere. Supreme goal of life not comfort, but character.
   III. **With us in trial.**
      A. **Doesn't promise never tried, but never alone**—vs. 4a. Principal difference between Christian and non-Christian is not that we never have rain, flood or wind, but that have something firm to stand on when comes (Matt. 7:24).

B. **Heals the hurting**—vs. 4c, 5a. Rods (holds back) each sheep as it enters fold at end of day. If scalp torn, dresses head with olive oil. Sheep are forever hurting each other and so are people. Injured can suffer in silence, bleat to others, or go to shepherd for healing.

IV. **Brings happiness.**
   A. **Refreshes weary**—vs. 5c. Weary sheep throws itself down in fold, panting. Shepherd fills his two-handled cup with water. Sheep thrusts muzzle deeply as water runs over sides. Water of life can refresh us as we worship today.
   B. **Leads to the good life**—vs. 6. Should be optimists. What bad thing ruin us if following Good Shepherd.

Conclusion

One hundred eighteen certain words in King James Version of Psalm 23. All certain except "my." He's Good Shepherd, but is He my shepherd? Dying child was taught Psalm 23 by pastor. Holding up boy's little hand, pastor assigned a word to each finger, "The Lord is my shepherd." When died, had hold of "my" finger.

512. Character Growth and the Christian

[Expository sermon outline of a chapter—John 6. Topic: sanctification.]

Introduction

John 6 called "great divide." At beginning of chapter crowds followed Jesus. At close many left Him. Disappointed because Jesus taught:

Theme: *Primary purpose of Christianity is to change us, not our circumstances.*

I. **Possible to follow Christ and be lost, if follow for wrong reasons.**
   A. **Followed Christ for His miracles**—John 6:24-26. We tempted follow Christ for what can get out of Him.
   B. **Disappointed in Christ when wouldn't give what wanted**—vs. 34. The more Christ does for selfish the more they want. For selfish, never enough miracles any more than enough money.
   C. **Hard love someone turns down.** Pray but baby stillborn, child handicapped, spouse cancer, mother stroke, turned down for job. When God says no we tend to one of two reactions:
      1. **I'm no good.** Something wrong with me. But goodness doesn't prevent trial. Lesson of Jesus' life is not that the Christian experiences no darkness, but that can succeed despite it.

    2. **God doesn't care.** Something wrong with God. We want omnipotent (all powerful) God who'll let us be omniscient (all wise). We make the decisions, He works the miracles. "I'll serve you and you make me feel good, protect me on highway, keep kids from going over fool's hill." When don't get own way disillusioned, "I'll quit believing—or never fully trust again."

  D. **Unfair to hold against God for failing to keep promises never made.** Doesn't promise protection from trial, but presence in trial, growth through trial, everlasting life—vs. 27a.

II. **Do not follow Christ just so He'll change circumstances.**

  A. **We don't know what we really need**—vs. 14, 15. Thought they needed king when really needed Savior.

  B. **We want Christ to change circumstances—He wants to change characters.** Life understood only backward, but must be lived forward. God's eternal dilemma how get people accept help they don't know they need.

III. **Follow Christ so He'll change you**—vs. 50, 53.

  Bread, flesh, blood work from within. We want Christ start working on people around us. Most problem is within us. His power works within Right reasons for following Christ:

  A. **Give self to Christ because He gave Himself to save you**—vs. 28, 29. They willing to work, He wanted them to believe. Price of heaven is Jesus. They willing pay any price except relationship.

  B. **Give self to Christ because He make into something world needs**—vs. 11. Little becomes much when placed in hands of Jesus.

Conclusion
Verses 66, 67 "You do not want to leave too, do you?"

513. Adventist Home Reform

[Expository sermon outline. Topic: home. Note exposition and segments. Concludes with poem.]

Introduction
I heard Dr. Ned Gaylin, sociologist, speaking at secular banquet say 10 commandments best foundation for society and that four of the 10 speak directly or indirectly about home. If true:

Theme: *Only home reformers are commandment keepers.*

I. **There's more home than Sabbath in 10 Commandments.**

SDAs emphasize commandment keeping, but tend to mean mostly Sabbath. If 40% of commandments deal with home, we not commandment keepers till home reformers.

Let's look at what four sociologist have said give foundation to a home:

II. **4th Commandment: Sabbath a day for family rest together.**
Ex. 20:10—seven resters mentioned, but parent, son and daughter mentioned first, mentioned together. Once family had to work together to survive. Now separate jobs all week. Family Sabbath togetherness needed now more than ever.

III. **5th Commandment: children, any age, responsibility parents**—vs. 12
   A. **Honor mothers**—in Sinai's world women used. God honored.
   B. **Honor hurting fathers and mothers.** They come to church with hearts aching, looking for comfort. We unconsciously tend to tell, "If had raised right, go right." They thought they had.
   C. **Honor aged.** Took care of his mother. Growing old isn't easy. Church has special need and comfort for elderly.

IV. **7th Commandment" adultery is still sin**—vs. 14.
When sex becomes more casual, becomes less meaningful, thus less joyful. God wants it to carry much meaning so bring much pleasure.

V. **10th Commandment: be content with the home you have**—vs. 17
"house" doesn't mean building so much as family.
   A. **Commandment breaking begins with desire, not act.** Most commandments emphasize act, 10th summarizes by emphasizing coveting, meaning compelling desire. Morality begins with right desires, clean thoughts.
   B. **Coveting another's spouse, a special temptation.** Why God so specific about it? Everybody mixture of good and bad. Bad so obvious in our own spouse, so hidden in neighbor's. Take appreciative look at what have rather than envy what haven't.

Conclusion
"Happy the home when God is there,
And love fills every breast;
When one their wish, and one their prayer,
And one their heavenly rest."
[Quote or sing remainder of the hymn.]

514. Christ and the Christian

[Expository-topical sermon outline. Studies whole gospel of John looking for symbols that help us love Christ.]

Introduction

Are you a Christian? May be church member, but so was Judas and he was lost. Christianity a relational religion, not based primarily belief, theory, church, but person.

Theme: *Christianity is loving Christ.*

We'll look in gospel written by one who loved him most, to find four metaphors that help us love Him more.

I. *Why* **we should have love relationship with Christ.**
   A. **He's sacrificial lamb—symbolizing forgiveness for sin.** John 1:29. If can take away sin of whole world, can handle mine.
   B. **He's passover lamb—symbolizing deliverance from sin.** John 19:14a, 16 shows Jesus crucified at Passover. Passover symbolized deliverance from bondage in Egypt. Sacrificial lamb forgives, Passover lamb frees. Christ has answer to both penalty and power of sin. Arms of cross point two directions: forgiveness past, victory future. Too many Christians have one-armed cross.
   C. **He's serpent—symbolizing healing of hurts left by sin.** John 3:14,15 refers to those bitten by snakes (Numbers 21). Moses' serpent represented Christ. Those who looked to Him healed. Getting hurt is regular part living. Can look at one who hurt, can suffer in bitterness, or look to Christ and be healed.
   D. **He's magnet—symbolizing His making religion attractive**. John 12:32. Christ draws **all** nationalities, colors, ages, personalities—*all kinds.*
II. **How we can have love relationship with Christ.** Establish love relationship with Christ much like anybody else:
   A. **Learn to love by spending time together.**
      Human love. When lovers little time together, assume little love
      Christian love—John 10:3. Good Shepherd wants spend whole day with sheep. Our busyness prevents intimate relationship.
   B. **Learn to love by talking together.**
      Human love. Without communication loved ones never get close
      Christian love—John 10:3b "sheep listen." Bible study and prayer.
   C. **Learn to love by going places together.**
      Human love can't prosper unless enjoy going to same places.
      Christian love—John 10:4. Lifestyle. Go only where He can go.

Conclusion

Every horse in parade controlled except one. Colt no bridle or rope. Entirely free of external control for followed mother. No distraction could entice him from side of one he loved.

515. The Forgotten Waterpot

[Expository sermon outline. Topic: soulwinning. Segments flow very naturally, almost chronologically from passage.]

Introduction

Christian longs to be Christlike. Never happen till soulwinner, for soulwinning was passion of Jesus' life.

Theme: *To be Christlike is to be a soulwinner.*

Illustrated by five lessons from the best soulwinning story ever told:
I. **To be Christ like is to go out of our way for the sake of others.**
John 4:3,4 "had to go through Samaria." Jews didn't go through Samaria. He went against convention for sake of soul. We worthy of being called soulwinners only if pay price of going out of way.
II. **To be Christlike is to work even when weary**—vs. 5-7.
Was noon. Probably on road since dawn, traveling 15-20 miles.
   A. **Physical needs get too much of our time**—vs. 8. Why did it take 12 people to carry enough food for 13? One could have done it. We have 12 times too much concern for physical.
   B. Meeting Jesus makes physical things seem less important—vs. 28-30. We willing leave water jar (everyday, mundane, physical tasks, tiredness at end of day) to become good news Christians?
III. **To be Christlike is to value the single soul.**—vs. 7a. Never let numbers blind to value Jesus puts on single soul. Worth lifetime of effort. Soulwinner is somebody who genuinely cares for *individuals.*
IV. **To be Christlike is to win others through kindness.**
   A. **Kindness attracts**—vs. 7, 9. Women usually came to well about 5 p.m. to talk, etc. She had probably been talked about. Came at noon to avoid unkindness. Jesus kindness surprised and attracted. Asking a favor flatters and makes people feel worthy.
   B. **Kindness reaching *down* social ladder most effective**. Jesus with Samaritan woman, youth with younger, employer with employee, successful with less successful. Our social climbing instinct stronger than desire to win souls.
V. **To be Christlike is to be an excitable soulwinner**—vs. 31-34.
Soulwinning turned Jesus on. Loved more than food.

Conclusion

Stranger in orange country wondered why no one picking. Orange pickers were organized showing where oranges were, computer files, committees, officers. Everybody so busy no time pick oranges. Drove away saying sadly "I have chosen you . . . that ye should go and bring forth fruit" (John 15:16, KJV).

516. Picking Up Stones? or People?

[Expository sermon outline. Topic: criticism. Divisions come directly from theme.]

Introduction
Sinner, Jesus and judges came together at temple. Seemed foolproof trap. John 8:4-6a. If Jesus told to stone it would be sedition against Rome. If let her go it would be heresy against Moses' church manual. What would Jesus do?

Theme: *Christ neither* condemns *sinners nor* condones *sin—He* convicts *and* converts.

We'll focus on above four words:
  I. **Christ does not condemn sinners**—vs. 11b.
     Criticism is exciting. It is self exalting. It isn't Christian.
 II. **Christ does not condone sin**—vs. 11c.
     A. **Jesus standards are high.**
        Higher than Pharisees who excused men and accused women.
        Higher than Moses—Matt. 5:31, 32.
        Went farther than 10 commandments—Matt. 5:27, 28. Beyond act to attitude. External sins serious, but internal sins destroy.
     B. **There is little merit in loving sinners if you love sin.** Easier to forgive sinners if don't think sin serious. Jesus hates sin too much to overlook, loves sinners to much to condemn for it.
III. **Christ convicts.**
     A. **Christ doesn't convict us of others' sins**—John 8:6b, 7. Sinners have no right to judge sins of others, not even if we couch it in nice words. Society condones putting knife in gently, cutting people up kindly.
     B. **To be in the presence of Christ is to be convicted of own sins.** Devil convicts of others sins. Holy Spirit convicts of own by prompting, "Am I doing anything I would condemn in others?"
 IV. **Christ converts.**
     A. **Offers hope for fallen**—vs. 9. When in crowd felt condemned. When alone with Jesus, forgiven (DA p. 462).
     B. **Offers hope for criticized**—vs. 10, 11. Go on from here. Don't let mistake or mistreatment lead to defeat, bitterness, self pity.
     C. **Offers hope for critic**—vs. 11c "leave your life of sin." You too are loved. You too can be forgiven.

Conclusion

When church establishes self as place of healing, not judgment, sin-sick will come. Let's not go out to pick up stones, but people.

517. Christ Cares

[Expository sermon outline. Exemplifies close exposition. Introduction begins with entire Bible passage.]

Introduction

John 5:1-10. Invalid's life was touched that day by three kinds of people: selfish who loved themselves, legalists who loved rules, Jesus who loved him. We relearn lesson he learned—

Theme: *Christ cares.*

- I. **Selfish who loved themselves.**
  - A. **All tempted to push ahead at expense of others**—vs. 7.
  - B. **Everyone in congregation should have someone**—vs. 7a.
  - C. **We grow in proportion to service we render others**. Selfish complain others don't make them happy. Happiness found by making others happy.
- II. **Legalists who loved rules.**
  - A. **Loved rules more than people**—vs. 10. Ok if bed carried man on Sabbath, but sinful if man healed and carried bed.
  - B. **Christ teaches rules are for helping people**—vs. 10b. Jesus purposely healed on Sabbath to teach Sabbath special time for miracles, healing.
- III. **Christ who loves people.**
  - A. **Christ loves helpless, hurting people**—vs. 5. Thirty-eight years of defeat proved every human help failed. But Christ succeeded.
  - B. **Wanting precedes healing**—vs. 6. Not easy question. People wouldn't sympathize anymore, nobody carry him, have go to work. Do we really want to be healed of our overindulgence, covetousness, sins, or just freed from their results?
  - C. **Christ's healing is as immediate as it is complete**—vs. 8, 9a. Justification complete in a moment. You can be rid of sins as quickly as he rid of bed.
  - D. **Christ expects healing to be followed by growth**—vs 14. Whom Christ heals, He longs to help grow. Sign at Arizona quicksand, "Safe so long as you keep moving."

Conclusion

The same Christ who cared about invalid's needs that day, cares about your needs today. He reaches down asking you just now, "Do you want to be made well?"

518. Made, Marred and Mended

[Expository sermon outline. Topic: success by yielding. Example of poem or hymn in conclusion.]

Introduction

God sent Jeremiah to potter to find an illustration. Lump on wheel began to form vessel, suddenly fell apart. Now what? God now ready to teach us the lesson—

Theme: *The life submitted to God cannot fail.*

I. **Living includes failing.**
   A. **Failure is with us all our lives**—Jer. 18:4a. [Examples of failures typical to child, youth, middle age, old age.]
   B. **Failure can quicken growth.** Winners forget most of their mistakes. We change most right after failure—either for better or worse. How failures can lead to success:

II. **First answer to failure: try again.**
   A. **Christ doesn't just make us *feel* good. He makes of us something that *is* good**—vs. 4b. Potter didn't just pick up clay and hold it. Does most good by kneading, pummeling, pressing against wheel.
   B. **Easy answer to failure, quit. God's answer, try again.** Good to know Christ never going give up on us. We may stop cooperating, but He never stops trying.
   C. **Try again, but not same old way.** Practice doesn't make perfect, just permanent. If try same old way likely experience same old failure.

III. **Second answer to failure: submit to God's plan for your life.**
   A. **God has a plan for your life**—vs. 4c. He'll give you everything you need to succeed at what He wants you to be.
   B. **Waste of time to complain about the kind of vessel you are**—Rom. 9:21. With Christ's help change what can change, accept what can't.
   C. **Usually fail because trying to be something not designed for.** Rom. 9:21b. Handpainted china may be prettier, but plain plate that goes to table every day may do greater service. Be whatever designed to be: a pen is good tool, but not to fix engine or drive nail. Hammer failure when tries to be screwdriver.

D. **Real secret to success is yielding**—Jer. 18:5, 6. No more reach
potential without Christ than clay become vessel without potter. [MH
p. 471] Christ shapes, we yield. But we may think yielding to Christ
when merely following our own mental convictions.

Farmer went on trip, leaving son to develop farm. Son built barn,
planted trees where father directed, but moved well down by barn
where he wanted. Father said didn't follow any of his directions,
for only place he disagreed, son followed his own plan. We only
know for sure we're willing to follow Christ's plan when He asks us
to do something we don't want to do.

Conclusion

In Eden, clay yielded. Foot didn't insist on being hand, nose an ear. When
finished, perfect man. How much more Christ make of us if really say,

"*Have Thine own way, Lord! Have Thine own way!*
Thou art the Potter; I am the clay.
Mold me and make me After Thy will,
While I am waiting, Yielded and still."

519. Christ's Church

[Expository, evangelistic sermon outline. Topic: 3 angels' messages. Same
illustration in introduction and conclusion for emphasis.]

Introduction

I walked into room filled with flags from all over world. [Demonstrate
with a flag if available.] Wanting to find the flag of my country I looked for
one that was red, white, blue; 50 stars; 13 stripes. There were many of right
color. Some had stars, some had stripes. But flag must have *all specifications*
to be my flag.

Rev. 14:14 describes Christ's Second Coming. The verses just before that,
depict 3 angels (heavenly messengers) giving 8 specifications of Christ's church
just before He comes. No church could be His church without *all specifications*.

Theme: *Christ's church must meet all Christ's specifications.*

First Angel.
I. **The everlasting gospel**—vs. 6a.
"Gospel" = good news of salvation through Christ.
"Everlasting" = not new beliefs, but original from Jesus, early church.
Boys helping father build shed. He gave pattern, but they sawed each
board according to last one. Two inches off. "Better get back to pattern."

II. **A mission-minded church**—vs. 6b.

Of 8 million SDAs, nearly 90% outside US where movement began.

III. **Judgment is here**—vs. 7a.

Most churches teach judgment—but in future. SDAs teach pre-Advent judgment going on now.

IV. **Worship God as Creator**—vs. 7b.

Even wording parallels Ex. 20:11. Sabbath a memorial of Creation.

Second Angel.

V. **Bible truth above church tradition**—vs. 8.

A. **Time tends to adulterate truth with tradition**. Babylon means confusion—caused when churches adulterate truth by mixing with tradition. Could 150 years have replaced some truths with tradition in Adventism? Example: if vegetarianism significant, why isn't exercise? Truth? or tradition?

B. **Only an ongoing study of Bible principles prevents tradition from replacing truth**. Any church whose members spend 10 hours TV for every 10 minutes Bible will gradually replace Bible truth with church tradition.

Third Angel.

VI. **Beware mark of beast**—vs. 9, 10a.

Dan. 7 and Rev. 12 identify as religious organization that "thinks to change times and laws." Beast represents power claiming right to change Sabbath to Sunday without scriptural authority.

VII. **Keep commandments**—vs. 12.

Love at heart of Christianity, but 10 commandments define what love is.

VIII. **Faithful to Jesus**—vs. 12c.

Law is standard, grace is method. "And" = Uniqueness of Adventism must be its balancing faith *and* obedience. Salvation's rowboat has two oars: faith and obedience. Using either without the other we just go in circles. To get anywhere must use both.

Conclusion

Does your church, do your personal beliefs include *all specifications?* [Return to flag] When I find flag that meets all specifications I want to give my life to it and for it.

520. He Comes

[Expository doctrinal sermon outline. Topic: Second Advent. Note close exposition.]

Introduction

Second Advent one of most mentioned truths—1,500 times—in Bible. Great time to be Adventist. Every generation since World War II assumed children better off than parents. No longer. When think getting better, tempted to stay here. When not, Jesus words sound better and better—John 14:1-3 "I *will*" not might or could.

Theme: *Let's be Adventists.*

I. **He comes.**
   A. **If you don't believe He'll come, maybe it's because you don't want Him to**—2 Peter 3:3, 4a But if our spiritual condition determines our beliefs, how will beliefs ever change condition?
   B. **Tempting argument: what has never been will never be**—vs. 4. He's never come, never destroyed so never will.
      But he has destroyed—vs 5-7. Flood a dress rehearsal for Advent. Shows He will destroy, kind of people destroyed, and escape available—ark then, Second Coming now.
         He has come in First Advent. Easier to believe He'll come in glory than that he would come to be born in a barn.
II. **He comes to destroy things.**
   A. **Everything destructible is unreal, unreliable**—vs. 10-12. Nuclear warfare makes easier to understand. We think what touch, count is real. Anything that can be destroyed by fire unreal: houses and cars, boats and RVs, checking accounts and insurance policies.
   B. **Everything indestructible is real, reliable.** Faith—fire cannot destroy. Character—can take to heaven, Christ—making indestructible home. Human craves security. When understand only spiritual indestructible our yearning for security attracts to.
III. **He comes to save people.**
   A. **If God gets His way you'll be saved**—vs. 9 "not wanting." God doesn't stand over daring sin so can destroy. Three votes for your soul: devil votes no, Christ yes, your vote breaks tie.
   B. **Salvation only through Christ's perfection**—vs. 13,14. None that good. But when Christ takes our blame, blameless. When His robe covers, spotless. And when blameless, spotless, we're at peace.

Conclusion
Let's be Adventists. Little girl climbed ladder leaned against house. Frightened, froze. "Look up, father coming." Father borrowed neighbor's ladder, put up on other side house, came over peak and rescued. Looking down scary. Keep looking up, Jesus is coming. Let's be Adventists.

521. How to Enjoy a Good Christian Experience

[Textual, doctrinal sermon outline. Topic: righteousness by faith.]

Introduction

Many who feel enjoy *good* Christian experience don't seem to *enjoy* their good Christian experience. Ps. 40:8—Psalmist came to where doing right became delight instead of duty. How?

Theme: *Happy (true) Christian is one who has found, not only something to believe, but someone to love.*

I. **In Adventism always been built-in temptation to legalism.**
   Hard if don't coffee, tobacco, pig to keep from thinking better than others. If keep commandments, tithe to keep from thinking cause salvation.
   A. **Uniqueness of Adventism should not be law, but balance**—Rev. 14:12. Ellen White warned from left ditch fanaticism, right legalism.
   B. **1888 Argument: faith alone or faith + works.** E. J. Waggoner took first stance, Uriah Smith the second. Which is right?
   Three steps to definition of righteousness by faith:

II. **Only Christ's righteousness sufficient.**
   Rom. 5:19—Perfect obedience required, but Christ's obedience. We (Adam) can lose selves, but not save selves. Saved by Christ's doing and dying, not by what we do, but what Christ did. Christ didn't indict badness so much as self righteousness. Our worst enemy not our badness but presumed goodness.

III. **Christ's righteousness becomes ours through faith (trust).**
   Eph. 2:8—Christ accepts, not because I'm good, but because He's good. Hard to understand, for life teaches **work precedes reward**. [Give personal examples of how taught by parents, teachers, bosses.] With Christ **reward precedes work.** It's natural to love someone that treats that much better than deserve.

IV. **Obedience then from love.**
   A. **Characteristic of disciple not good deeds, good motives**—Ps. 40:8. Teenage boy won't wash or comb hair. Falls for girl and can't get him out of bathroom. Love makes him want to do what once hated to do.
   B. **Cheap grace insufficient.** Righteousness by faith doesn't remove need for self discipline. Easier do good deeds than have good relationships, obey boss than love, stay married than stay in love. Relationships require hard work, but pleasant if love.

Conclusion

Good works are not cause, but *fruit* of salvation (Gal. 5:22, 23). Don't get apples by tying them on tree. They might look good, but soon dry up and fall off. There's work in growing apples, but the principal work is digging the hole and planting the tree. Planted trees just naturally produce apples. Rooted in Christ, good works follow.

522. Why Keep the Sabbath?

[Topical, doctrinal sermon outline. First in a two part series on Sabbath. Note each division is a question followed by an answer.]

Introduction

I built a swing in our backyard not because of need within me, but need within my child—Mark 2:27. Sabbath for God's children.

Theme: *The Sabbath was made for* us—*God gave it because* we *need.*

Why do we need? Answers the three great questions of life:
I. **Where did I come from?**
    Sabbath reminds us we were made by God for fellowship with God.
    A. **Made by God**—Ex. 20:11a "all that is in them" includes me. Sabbath shows God can make something of nothing. Memorial not just what did creation week, but this week, for creates daily.
    B. **Made for fellowship with God**—Ex. 20:11b. Only commandment God joins us in observing. God rested, man rests—meeting place of God and man. He didn't spend Sabbath with anteaters and elephants, but in fellowship with Adam and Eve.
II. **Why am I here?**
    Sabbath reminds completeness requires both physical and spiritual.
    A. **Sabbath made especially for humans because only humans have spiritual dimension.** Grass, birds, horses never worship.
    B. **Sabbath a sign God can make holy**—Eze. 20:12. Sit in church, "If God make day, building, other people holy, can make me holy too." God loves people more than time. If willing make time holy surely willing make me holy.
    C. **Every Sabbath I learn what runs my life**—Eze. 20:20 "Lord" When I decide do my own thing on Sabbath, saying "I'm Lord."
III. **Where am I going?**
    Sabbath promises a restored creation. Is. 66:22, 23. Sabbath reminds we're not home yet. Nature walk we see beauty reminding of heaven; also dying trees, wilting flowers, dead things that remind we're not home yet. As we

worship we learn of pain in church family, reminds not home yet where no pain, death, sorrow. But also that the way creation once was, it will be again.

Conclusion

Pennsylvania mines brought mules out of darkness to sunlight once week or go blind. This Sabbath God wants bring us out of world's darkness to see light of Creator's face so spiritual blindness healed. Sabbath was made for us. We need it. Let's use it.

523. How to Keep the Sabbath

[Topical-expository, doctrinal sermon outline. Second in a 2 part series on Sabbath. Includes a visual aid.]

Introduction

First Sabbath began as sunset painted sky with beauty, filling Adam and Eve with joy. Every Sabbath since begun with setting sun to associate with joy and beauty.

Theme: *We really keep the Sabbath only when we enjoy it.*

Gen. 2:1-3 "rested . . . blessed . . . holy". These three words give three proofs the Sabbath was meant to be enjoyed:

I. **Sabbath is a *rest* day.**
   A. **God created rest that's more than physical**—vs. 2a. Thank God for last thing He created—rest. More than physical, for God rested and He doesn't need physical. Girl looks forward to boy coming for date, but he promptly falls asleep, "I'm too busy to sleep on my time. I'll sleep on your time."
   B. **Sabbath not rest day unless work finished before day begins**— Ex. 16:23-26. Everything possible should be prepared. If friends coming for party, insult to wait till arrive to prepare. Incidentally, also impolite keep looking at watch hoping visit over.
   C. **God forbids *all* work on Sabbath**—Ex. 20:8-10a. Work is what we'd stop doing if stopped getting paid.

II. **Sabbath is a happy day.**
   Gen. 2:3a "blessed" means happy.
   A **Sabbath meant to be a delight**—Is. 58:13, 14a. Satan has two Sabbath tactics: not keep, or keep in way can't enjoy. [Illustrate with 7 glasses, 6 plain water, 1 brightly colored.] Sabbath special.
   B. **If Sabbath is family time, children will remember it as happy time.** Gen. 2:23,24—last thing created before Sabbath was home. Sabbath

is family time. Doing nothing is treat to you but boredom to kids. Provide some family-centered privileges available only on Sabbath (MH 307).

III. **Sabbath is a holy day.**
   A. **Holy means having God present**—Gen. 2:3a. Bush, Sinai, ark holy when God in. Presence of air makes rubber into raft—no air, no raft. Presence of God makes time into Sabbath.
   B. **Love demands time together.** In courtship learn to love each other by spending time together. Sabbath is time spent with God.

Conclusion

Everybody loves Mother's Day if love mother. Everybody can learn to love God's special day if love God. We really keep Sabbath only when enjoy it because we love Him.

524. Spirit of Prophecy

[Topical, doctrinal sermon outline. Topic: Spirit of Prophecy. Includes visual aid.]

Introduction

December, 1844. Five women met in prayer band. One was Ellen Harmon, 17-years old, 5-foot 2-inches tall, 80 pounds. As prayed she claimed vision. Later married James White. For 70 years did work of prophet in church. Was hard for me appreciate: modern prophet, woman preacher. In college I studied deeper and became convinced. Want share why.

Theme: *Five reasons I believe Ellen White was God's prophet:*

I. **Bible predicted.**
   A. **Spirit of Prophecy to continue to end of time**—Eph. 4:11-13. Prophecy the only gift in all three major lists of spiritual gifts (Rom. 12, 1 Cor. 12, Eph. 4). All permanent in church.
   Rev. 12:17, 19:10—a special sign of remnant church.
   B. **Always special messenger for every special movement.** [Have two men and two women stand beside you.] When going to *destroy* by flood first called prophet to warn. (Noah step forward.) When going to *deliver* from Egypt, (Moses step forward). When calling from *idolatry* called woman, (Deborah step forward). To announce *First Advent* called another woman, (Anna step forward). At Second Advent going to destroy, deliver, call from idolatry, announce advent. If God used prophet similar circumstances, expect now.

II. **Her life and teachings.**
Matt. 7:15,20—know prophets by fruits. 1 John 4:1-3a—must teach Christ. Does in all books, especially *Desire Ages, Steps Christ.*

III. **What done for church.**
Helped perfect worldwide organization with wholistic program. Guarded against fanaticism by warning away from emotionalism on one hand and legalism on other. Only way can harm church rather than help is if replaces Bible or used in harsh discipline. We trained pup by swatting with newspaper when misbehaved. Rest of her life she hated newspaper and ran whenever unfolded. Don't like what punished with.

IV. **Condition in vision.**
Not only supernatural, but like Daniel 10 (strength, no breath), Numbers 24 (Balaam trance, eyes open). [Tell stories of her condition in vision.]

V. **Makes me a better person.**
2 Chron. 20:20c—helps succeed spiritually. High standard, but not fanatical. Try reading *Steps Christ, Thoughts From the Mount of Blessings, The Desire of Ages, Christ Object Lessons.*

Conclusion

My college classmate blind but finished course because helped by friend who was her "seer." Prophets called "seers." Let Ellen White help you see the way to finishing your course.

525. Change and the Church

[Topical sermon outline. Topic: change in church. Can work as youth sermon. An inductive development, with theme late in sermon rather than in introduction.]

Introduction

Adventism began in days of horse drawn carriages, lantern light. Fit age computers, space ships? Should change to fit times? Let's talk about change:

I. **Change is resisted.**
Humans resist change and churches tend to especially resist it. Rev. 3:17. Mark of Laodicea is not knowing needs change. We resist change even in order of worship service.

II. **Change is divisive.**
Pits progressive against conservative, old against young. Old: "Stay by landmarks." Young: "Don't press 19th century practices on us approaching 21st century"

III. **Change is necessary.**

A. **Life is change.** Any religion that prepares us for life must prepare us to meet change, for life is change. Mothers illustrate. Child moves from total intimacy and dependence in womb to almost total independence as leaves home to be intimate with another woman. Such total change hard for mother to handle, but life is change.

B. **Church is changing.** Rev. 14:6 has led to ethnic change in make- up of church. 89% SDAs live outside NAD. 70% of all SDAs are in Africa, Latin America or South America. Difficult for majority to become minority graciously. Almost nobody volunteers to give up power.

IV. **Change is Christian.**

A. **God changes His way of working.** We quote Mal. 3:6, yet God has used 3 different organizations: patriarchal, national (Israel), church. His example shows church change to remain contemporary.

B. **Jesus didn't emphasize political (coercive, external) change**—Matt. 5:39-41. Taught effective change comes from love, not coercion. Said His kingdom works like yeast, from inside out. We change world by first changing ourselves.

C. **Jesus did emphasize change when tradition placed it above principle.**

    Changed worship tradition by cleansing temple—John 2:15-17. Would not stand for worship leaders taking advantage of worshipers.

    Changed social tradition by going through Samaria and talking to questionable woman there.

    Changed Sabbath tradition by healing on Sabbath 6 times—Mark 2:27.

    Jesus changed tradition to protect principle. His lesson—

Theme: *Traditions & rules must change, principles must never change.*

V. **Change rules and traditions—protect principles.**

A. **Principle is fundamental, timeless truth**—Matt. 22:35-40. Everything hangs on love to God, love to man.

B. **Rules control behavior**—not what believe, only how act. Can control behavior all life and not teach principle. Rules change:

    Ellen White advised women about hemlines that dragged on ground, "Up." Dormitory deans advise about hemlines, "Down." Rules opposite, to teach same principles of health and modesty.

C. **Human tendency is to gradually substitute rules and traditions for principles.** Jesus called such worship vain—Matt. 15:9. Every church and every Christian needs to continually look for the principles lest traditions replace them. Christianity based on principle is never out of date.

Conclusion

For centuries people lighted homes with same kind of oil, but each generation carried it in lamps of contemporary design. Oil represents principle. Never dilute oil. Lamps represent way principles are applied to contemporary world. May the old be as willing to fight for new lamps as instinctively fight for old oil. May the young be as willing to fight for old oil as instinctively fight for new lamps.

526. Hyperopia

[Biographical/narrative sermon outline especially adapted to youth. Topic: spiritual farsightedness.]

Introduction

Hyperopia is a $100 word for farsightedness. Shortsighted people often in trouble: child walks through mud puddles and gets cold, youth chooses easiest work for highest pay but not fulfilled.

Farsighted people admired. Moses was farsighted—Heb. 11:24-26.

Theme: *We can succeed in life only when we focus on its ultimate, not just its immediate rewards.*

I. **Moses chose ultimate.**
   He could have had everything world offers. Was good looking (Heb. 11:23a), educated (Acts 7:22), physical ability to kill taskmaster. God called—Heb. 11:24, 25. A masochist? No, looked at ultimate rather than immediate rewards.
   Look first at immediate then ultimate results working for God:
II. **Immediate result of Moses' choice—sacrifice.**
   A. **Physical discomfort.** Left feather beds Egypt, 80 years sleeping in sand. No property, nomad all life. Some dying be missionaries if no language or snakes, have indoor plumbing and come home whenever tired of it. Christ never ask greater discomfort than cross. Goal in life not comfort but character.
   B. **Hard work**—Ex. 18:13. No guaranteed 8 hour days, 40 hour weeks.
   C. **Criticism and disappointment.** Israel forever complaining how God did His work—no wonder didn't approve how Moses did his.
III. **Ultimate result of Moses' choice—success.**
   A. **Physical blessing**—Deut. 34:7. Gods we worship write their names on our faces. Those who live for love become more attractive all their lives.
   B. **Accomplishment.** Kept a million people alive and brought to

Promised Land. Only mountain climber who climbs gets to see the view.
C. **Became Godlike**—Ex. 34:29, 30. Become like those we work with.
D. **Eternal life.** If chosen immediate results, he'd be leathered skeleton in museum today. But he's alive, at home with his Lord.

Conclusion

William Booth knelt in England chapel volunteering himself for service. Went out to form Salvation Army. Young American soldier asked to see place where Booth had knelt. Soldier knelt same spot and prayed, "O God, do it again." As see Moses who lived to give, his life centered on service, "O God, do it again." Succeed in life only as focus on ultimate, not immediate rewards.

527. The Widow's Might

[Special event expository sermon outline for Stewardship Sabbath. Notice almost the same visual aid is used at beginning and ending, for sake of emphasis.]

Introduction

[Have 10 apples and an apple core. Place each on table at appropriate time.] Once there was a man who had nothing. Because God loved, gave him three apples to eat, three to trade for clothing and shelter, three for miscellaneous needs, one to show gratitude to God. Used three eat, three clothing, three miscellaneous, but decided he needed the 10th also. Besides, God had all apples in world. Ate apple and gave God core.

Jesus watched as they took offering one day and taught—

Theme: *What we give depends more on what we are than what we have.*

Let's look at the story in four parts:
I. **Christ measures us by our giving.**
Mark 12:41. Tuesday of Passion week. One of last lessons he taught was about money. Half His teachings on money, more than faith and prayer combined, for knew tendency to covetousness. Two occasions when possessions dwindle: tax time and offering time. Emphasized giving for shrivels covetousness. Leg muscle in cast weakens. Muscle exercised strengthens. We have some givingness, some covetousness. Whichever we exercise grows strongest.
II. Christ measures us by whether our first love is people or things.
Mark 12:41a; 13:1. Jesus saw people, disciples saw things. What we see

in world: people to be helped? or things to be owned? To carnal nature wealth is in things, to Christian its in relationships. Sonny wanted skates. Mother said couldn't afford. "Are you poor?" "No, I have you and Billy. I'm rich." "Then mortgage Billy and buy me skates." Loved skates more than brother.

III. **Christ measures us by where we look for heaven.**
Mark 12:42,43. Widows exemplary givers for learned heaven isn't here. Heaven isn't in capsule, bottle, Joe Camel, theater, refrigerator, Detroit. Invest in the only heaven that works.

IV. **Christ measures us by who gets the leftovers.**
Mark 12:43,44. Christ not impressed by amount of money, but amount of sacrifice. Leftovers are for dogs, not God.

Conclusion
[Repeat 10 apples as at beginning except:] Because loved God, smaller car, simpler life, so used only 2 for miscellaneous and had 2 to give to God. Jesus smiled. Man smiled. He was content. What we give depends more on what we are than what we have.

528. Born in a Barn

[Special event expository sermon outline for Christmas season. Example of an introduction beginning with text.]

Introduction
Luke 2:7-12. "How tell which baby is Jesus?" "He'll be only one born in barn." Barns not beautiful but became beautiful symbol—

Theme: *Jesus can make anything beautiful.*

Four lessons from Bethlehem barn:
I. **Success depends less on the kind of place a person's in than on the kind of person that's in the place.**
A. **World makes way for the heart that's full of love.** If Jesus could make it from a barn, you can make it from where you are. Luke 3:1, 2a lists pomp, power, prestige. World trembled when spoke. Barn baby became strongest voice. Love stronger than force.
B. **Successful presents depend less on money in the bank than love in the heart.** Best Christmas present wife ever got from husband was box with little notes on which he'd written gifts redeemable upon request: one walk together, doing dishes, night out, one big hug.

II. **Jesus doesn't shun dirty places.**
Barns are dirty places. First odor God's son smelled was manure. But it was ideal place to be born, for Jesus comes only to dirty places. Don't try clean up before let Jesus in. If lost, not because too dirty, but because thought could make self clean.

III. **Jesus presence attracts.**
Luke 2:15,16. Nobody ever came to see stable, but did come to see Jesus. When others see Jesus in us they'll find us attractive.

IV. **God gives bountifully—mankind gives grudgingly.**
   A. **When mankind came into world, God gave His best.** Creator worked for 6 days and at end each day smiled, "They'll like that."
   B. **When God came into world mankind gave Him leftovers**—Luke 2:7c. Jesus placed where usually put cow feed. Barn was leftover after motel full and everybody else got what wanted. God giving you His best: Son, forgiveness, eternal life. Probably: family, friends, measure health, degree prosperity. You giving God leftovers: leftover love, money, time? Give God your best.

Conclusion

Bret Harte wrote story of California mining camp where only one woman. She died in childbirth but they saved baby. Put in middle bunkhouse but didn't seem right so sent Sacramento for rosewood cradle; entire layette, frills and all. Didn't seem enough so scrubbed floors, whitewashed walls, curtained windows, even cleaned selves up. Camp transformed by birth baby. Let Jesus be born in your heart this Christmas—change from filthy to clean, selfish to loving, worried to contented. Jesus can make anything beautiful.

529. In the Beginning, God

[Special event textual sermon outline for New Years Communion. Topic: putting God first.]

Introduction

Let's begin new year with the four words beginning Bible—Gen 1:1a "In the beginning God." When week began with God, what a week it was: order where had been chaos, light where darkness, life where nothing. What a year this year can be if God in beginning: of every day, every decision, every family problem; our finances, our time.

Theme: *In the beginning, God.*

Paul shows us what it means—Phil 3:13,14. Says means three things:

I. **Simplifying your life**—Phil. 3:13b "one thing I do"—single-mindedness. We have too many things do, places go, people please. God first doesn't take away all busyness but simplifies life, minimizes stress.

II. **Forgetting your failures**—vs. 13b "forgetting what is behind." At after-Christmas sales this time of year merchants get rid of unwanted merchandise.

      Communion wine says, when forgiven, we're rid of unwanted past. There'll not be one single day of 1996 in 1997.

III. **Anticipating future**—vs. 13c,14a "straining toward what is ahead, I press on toward the goal." Paul was sports fan. He says runner eagerly anticipates goal.

      Communion bread says Christian eagerly anticipates future. Bread is called "staff of life." Represents source of strength. When take bread, taking Christ's strength, into my body. His strength becomes my strength. Anticipating victory I face the future eagerly, expectantly. Task ahead of me not nearly so great as Christ's power within me.

Conclusion

As new year confronts us let's begin it with God so can say,

> *"Many things about tomorrow,*
> *I don't know or understand.*
> *But I know who holds tomorrow,*
> *And I know who holds my hand."*

Task ahead of us never as great as power behind us.

530. He Is Risen!

[Special event topical/expository sermon outline for Communion during Easter season. Topic: sinners come first.]

Introduction

Some celebrate Jesus resurrection with fancy clothes, painted eggs and furry rabbits. Can lose sight of Jesus even in celebrating His resurrection. Real resurrection story in Mark 16:1-6. Notice whom He came to first—

Theme: *With risen Lord sinners come first.*

I. **Sinners came first at resurrection.**
   A. **Jesus came to Mary Magdalene first**—Mark 16:9. Why? Of all the people Jesus loved she branded greatest sinner. Came to her first to let us know that, with risen Lord sinners come first.
   B. **Jesus sent word to Peter first**—vs. 7. Why? Peter backslidden, denied

Lord publicly, looked on self as almost unforgivable sinner. With risen Lord sinners come first.

II. **Sinners come first today.**

    A. **Never know thrill of being saved till known misery of being lost.** Luke 15:18,19—Prodigal never knew the thrill of home until he saw himself as unworthy of it.

    B. **Hiding fact of our sinfulness fools no one but ourselves.** Little girl played hide-and-seek by shutting her eyes, presuming if she couldn't see others they couldn't see her. We do that with sins. As though shutting our eyes to our sins would mean they aren't there.

Conclusion

Sweet pea package pictures gorgeous blossoms, but inside are just wrinkled little pellets. Planting is process by which ugly seed becomes beautiful flower. Communion illustrates process by which, through forgiveness of Jesus represented by wine, strength of Jesus represented by bread, we change from ugly sinners to beautiful children of God. Won't you let Him make that change in you?

Bibliography

Abbey, Merrill R. *The Epic of United Methodist Preaching*. New York: University Press of America, 1984.

Anderson, Roy Allen. *Preachers of Righteousness*. Nashville, Tennessee: Southern Publishing Association, 1963.

Beecher, Henry Ward. *Yale Lectures on Preaching*. New York: Ford, 1972.

Beekman, John and Callow, John T. *Translating the Word of God*. Grand Rapids: Zondervan Publishing House, 1974.

Bradford, Charles E. *Preaching to the Times*. Silver Spring, MD: General Conference SDA Ministerial Association, 1994.

Brooks, Phillips. *Lectures on Preaching*. New York: Dutton, 1877.

Brown, David. *Dramatic Narrative in Preaching*. Valley Forge, PA: Judson Press, 1981.

Brown, H. C. *A Christian Layman's Guide to Public Speaking*. Nashville: Broadman Press, 1966.

Cook, Alvin E. *Preach the Word*. Makwasa, Malawi: Malamulo Publishing House, 1973.

Day, Richard Ellsworth. *The Shadow of the Broad Brim*. Takoma Park, Washington DC: Review and Herald Publishing Assn., 1942.

Foley, Nadine, editor. *Preaching and the Non-ordained*. Collegeville, Minn.: The Liturgical Press, 1983.

France, Richard. "Which Version is Best?" *Ministry Magazine*, August, 1972.

GC Ministerial Association, unpublished *paper, Ordination, a Statement, 1988*.

Haynes, Carlyle B. *The Divine Art of Preaching*. Washington D. C.: Review and Herald, 1939.

Howe, Reuel L. *Partners in Preaching*. New York: Seabury, 1967.

Jabusch, Willard F. *The Person in the Pulpit: Preaching as Caring*, ed. W. D. Thompson. Nashville: Abingdon, 1980.

Jeffs, Harry. Practical Lay Preaching and Speaking to Men. London: James Clarke and Co., 1907.

————. *Progressive Lay Preaching*. London: James Clarde and Co., Limited, 1924.

Knight, George. *Millennial Fever*. Boise, Idaho: Pacific Press Publishing Association, 1993.

Morrow, Thomas M. *Worship and Preaching*. London: The Epworth Press, 1956.

Nida, Eugene. *Toward the Science of Translating*. Leiden: E. J. Brill, 1964.

Osgood, Charles. *Osgood on Speaking*. New York, NY: William Morrow and Co., 1989.

Pearce, Winston. *Planning Your Preaching*. Nashville: Broadman Press, 1967.

Perry, Lloyd M. *Biblical Sermon Guide*. Grand Rapids: Baker Book House, 1970.

Pollard, Leslie N. *Increasing the Persuasive Power of Your Preaching*. Unpublished paper, Berrien Springs, MI, 1992.

Richards, H. M. S. *Feed My Sheep*. Washington D. C.: Review and Herald Pub. Assoc., 1958.

Seventh-day Adventist Elder's Handbook. Silver Spring, MD: General Conference Ministerial Association, 1994.

Stott, John R. W. *Between Two Worlds: The Art of Preaching in the Twentieth Century*. Grand Rapids, MI: William B. Eerdmans, 1982.

Sweazey, George. *Preaching the Good News*. Englewood Cliffs, NJ: Prentice-Hall, 1976.

Thompson, William D. *A Listener's Guide to Preaching*. Nashville: Abingdon Press, 1966.

Turnbull, Ralph G. *A History of Preaching, vol. 3*. Grand Rapids, MI.: Baker Book House, 1974.

Von Allmen, J. J. *Preaching and Congregations*. London: Lutterworth Press, 1962.

White, Ellen G. *Education*. Mountain View, Calif.: Pacific Press Publishing Association, 1942.

————. *Gospel Workers*. Washington, DC: Review and Herald Publishing Assn., 1948.

————. *Great Controversy*. Mountain View, Calif.: Pacific Press Publishing Association, 1950.

————. *Ministry of Healing*. Mountain View, Calif.: Pacific Press Publishing Association, 1942.